THE STORY OF MEXICO

Modern Mexico

THE STORY OF MEXICO

Modern Mexico

R. CONRAD STEIN

Greensboro, North Carolina

The Story of Mexico: Modern Mexico
Copyright © 2012 by R. Conrad Stein

Morgan Reynolds Publishing, Inc.
620 South Elm Street, Suite 387
Greensboro, NC 27406 USA

Library of Congress Cataloging-in-Publication Data

Stein, R. Conrad.
The story of Mexico. Modern Mexico / by R. Conrad Stein. -- 1st ed.
    p. cm.
Includes bibliographical references and index.
ISBN 978-1-59935-162-9
1. Mexico--History--1910-1946--Juvenile literature. 2.
Mexico--History--1946---Juvenile literature. 3. Mexico--Politics and
government--1910-1946--Juvenile literature. 4. Mexico--Politics and
government--1946---Juvenile literature. I. Title. II. Title: Modern Mexico.

 F1234.S845 2012
972.08'4--dc22

                                2010053630

Printed in the United States of America
First Edition

Book Cover and interior designed by:
Ed Morgan, navyblue design studio
Greensboro, N.C.

For my wife, Deborah, and daughter, Janna

THE STORY OF MEXICO

TABLE OF CONTENTS

Rebels with a homemade cannon during the Mexican Revolution in 1911

CHAPTER 1

Aftermath of a Revolution

After ten years of unrelenting warfare, Mexico was an exhausted land. Towns were ruined and weeds covered the fields. The Mexican Revolution was a bitter conflict that pitted the rich against the poor and the landowners against the landless. The war raged from 1910 to 1920, unleashing a storm of hatred and violence. At least 1 million and perhaps as many as 2 million Mexicans died during the fighting and from the famine and disease brought about by warfare. This grim casualty figure dwarfed even the United States' Civil War of the 1860s, making the Mexican Revolution the deadliest clash of arms to ever take place on the American continent. No dramatic last battle ended the war. Instead the fighting slowed and finally stopped like an automobile running out of gasoline. The Mexican people were simply too tired to carry the war another step. There was no more blood left to spill.

To the outside observer it seemed as if the brutal war resolved nothing. The rich retained their fortunes and their land. The poor remained poor, and they owned almost nothing. Yet a subtle change had settled upon the nation.

Mexico had long supported a caste system based on race. Whites of European heritage (mostly Spanish) held the wealth and the political power. Mixed-race people (mestizos) were granted meager privileges by the white-ruling class. Indians were at the bottom of the system and were routinely denied rights.

The Mexican people emerged from the Revolution like survivors of an earthquake. They were dazed and stunned, but walked away from the calamity holding hands with fellow survivors. Though economic inequalities based on race remained, now no door was closed to anyone. All men and women were Mexicans. An astute observer of this transformation was Frank Tannenbaum, an American sociologist who lived in Mexico in the 1920s. Tannenbaum wrote, "The chief by-product of the Revolution is, therefore, spiritual, a discovery by the Mexican people of their own dignity."

The end of the Revolution (Mexican writers always capitalize the word Revolution because the upheaval was such a pivotal event) ushered in the era of modern Mexico, a time of tremendous social progress as well as discouraging setbacks. Strides were made in educating the mass of people, and Mexican culture spread throughout the world thanks to its food, artwork, cinema, and music. However, the Mexican economy suffered frustrating rises and falls. Always the United States, the powerful neighbor to the north, influenced Mexico's destiny.

An 1861 map shows Mexico and the United States

General Alavaro Obregón (front, center)
addresses a crowd in Mexico City in 1920

CHAPTER 2

The Search for Stability

In the spring of 1920 an army of 40,000 horsemen entered Mexico City and marched down the broad, tree-lined Reforma Boulevard. This was not a triumphant parade celebrating a glorious victory. Instead the march was a military show-of-force aimed at telling all revolutionaries that the fighting in Mexico was over.

Leading the parade was Alvaro Obregón, a no-nonsense army officer who had been the most successful general during the revolutionary fighting. Like many others, Obregón entered the war hoping to bring justice and prosperity to Mexico. Now his only goal was to establish order. He believed the high ideals of the Mexican Revolution would have to wait to be applied in more secure times. His countrymen echoed his beliefs. The decade from 1910 to 1920 was the most devastating ten-year span in the nation's history. Now Mexicans yearned for peace.

In his youth Âlvaro Obregón was a chickpea farmer from the state of Sonora. An amateur mechanic, he invented a chickpea planting machine which he patented and sold to fellow farmers. When the Mexican Revolution broke out he joined the anti-government forces and took command of a troop of Yaqui Indians. He quickly won the Yaquis' confidence and respect. Obregón had little formal education, but he was a voracious reader. He studied the battle techniques of great generals of the past such as Napoleon and Alexander the Great. As a commander, he applied the techniques he learned in history books to the warfare of the Mexican Revolution and won battle after battle.

Obregón emerged from the war as a popular leader who had suffered for his country. In a 1915 battle near the city of León, shrapnel from an artillery shell tore off his right arm. General Obregón was covered with blood and in such intense pain he believed only death could end his suffering. He later wrote, "With the hand that was left to me, I drew my pistol . . . and shot at my left temple, trying to finish the work that the shrapnel had not." The gun failed to fire and quick medical attention saved the general's life. Afterward, Mexicans looked upon his severed limb as a badge of courage and dedication to his country.

In 1920, to no one's surprise, Obregón was elected president of Mexico. From the beginning he deemed it his goal to bring stability to the war-torn land. Obregón ruled in a time when violence simmered just below the surface of Mexican society. The country teemed with generals who wanted more power. President Obregón silenced the malcontents with policies ranging from conciliation to intimidation. Generals were put on government payrolls and given land and influence in their territories. All Obregón asked of the military strongmen was that they maintain the peace. Those officers who continued to agitate for greater rewards were treated harshly. Obregón did not hesitate to have rebellious generals brought before court-martial boards which sentenced them to be shot by a firing squad.

One general who accepted generous rewards was Pancho Villa, the one-time bandit chief turned revolutionary. During the war, General Villa was feared by all sides because of his aggressiveness and courage. In battle Villa led fierce calvary charges. Always he headed the horsemen personally and with his pistols blazing. After the war Villa was offered a large ranch in northern Mexico if he would simply disband his private army and live as a peaceful citizen. Villa agreed and took control of property spreading over more than 26,000 acres.

Perhaps the land grant was too generous. Landless farmers began moving on to the fringes of Villa's ranch and squatting there illegally. Just a few years earlier Villa fought in the name of such impoverished farmers. Now that the peasant farmers imposed on his land, Villa became furious. He hired thugs to gun down the squatters. The families of those who were killed swore revenge.

Pancho Villa

On July 20, 1923, Villa drove in a car through the northern Mexico town of Canutillo. An old man who sat on a sidewalk selling candy waved at him. Villa smiled at the elderly man. He did not know the wave was a signal to hidden gunmen who waited on rooftops across the street. Suddenly a roar of gunfire burst out. Sprayed by scores of bullets, Villa was killed instantly. Mexicans wondered who was behind the assassination. Many believed the murder was a government plot that had the approval of President Obregón. The president, who was no admirer of Pancho Villa, denied having any part of the assassination. Villa had made many enemies among the peasants who once adored him and perhaps he was murdered by the embittered farmers. Villa's death remains a mystery to this day.

Emiliano Zapata (1879-1919)

Pancho Villa's place in history is questioned: was he a true revolutionary or was he simply a bandit chief? There are no such questions in the hearts of Mexicans regarding another revolutionary general, Emiliano Zapata. Tirelessly Zapata fought to bring land ownership to the landless farmers of southern Mexico. "Land and Liberty" was his wartime slogan, and he acted true to those words. On April 10, 1919, Zapata was killed when ambushed by gunmen. But in the south it was believed he never died. Many farmers (campesinos) claimed they saw him years later riding at night on a great white horse. Always, said the campesinos, he was riding alone.

By necessity President Obregón ruled the nation in a stern manner, reminding many of a previous chieftain who became a demon in the minds of the people. Porfirio Díaz was Mexico's president for more than thirty years. He first took office in 1876 after civil wars and military revolts had rocked Mexico for decades. Díaz brought order to the country through a policy of *pan o palo* (bread or the club). The policy told ambitious military men and politicians that if you work with me you will be rewarded (bread); if you work against me then you will be struck down (the club). Porfirio Díaz reigned until 1910 when the people rebelled and the Mexican Revolution began.

To many citizens, the postwar presidency of Obregón looked eerily like the dictatorship of Díaz. But Obregón was by no means a carbon copy of Díaz. He hoped to see Mexico become a prosperous democracy some day. However, he was always the realist. Obregón believed the scars of war still ran deep in Mexico. He felt that democratic reforms in this unstable society had to be introduced gradually and piece-by-piece or warfare would explode again like a bomb with a simmering fuse.

Mexico was governed by rules laid down in the Constitution of 1917, a document that remains in force to this day. Written during the heat of war, the Constitution contained remarkably progressive measures. It called for freedom of religion and freedom of the press. Such basic rights were unheard of in the old days when Mexico was a Catholic country by law and was ruled by various dictators. One article gave Mexican workers the right to organize unions; another article banned child labor. No other nation in the world had the rights and privileges of workers written directly into its Constitution.

Though the Constitution of 1917 set high standards, much of its noble language was ignored after the Revolution. The country's leaders believed stability and the restoration of national order was more important than the freedoms promised by the Constitution. Often the Constitution was thought of as a statement of goals to be obtained in the future rather than a list of laws to be applied now.

Obregón's term in office expired in 1924. His was the first successful and largely peaceful presidency since the start of the Revolution.

Before retiring he handpicked his successor, another ex-general named Plutarco Elías Calles.

Calles was a grim-faced man, known to rarely smile and never laugh. He grew up under middle-class circumstances in the state of Sonora. There he came to believe his life was cursed because he was an illegitimate child; his father never married his birth mother. This meant Calles was an outcast in middle-class society. Laws denied him a proper inheritance from deceased relatives because he was an illegal offspring. He blamed the Catholic Church and its moral teachings for his diminished status. As a youth Calles went to church because the adults in his family required him to do so, but he once admitted, "When I was an altar boy as a child, I stole the alms to buy candy." Briefly he served as a school teacher. He was dismissed after parents of his students complained he spent classroom time ranting against the evils of the church instead of teaching the students reading and arithmetic.

The Catholic church had a long and often controversial history in Mexico. Spaniards brought Catholic teachings to Mexico in the 1500s. New Spain, as the country was then called, became a Catholic nation. Always the church had a stormy image because priests tended to side with the government against poor people and against those who called for change. There were notable exceptions to this pattern. The priest Miguel Hidalgo was a leader in the Mexican War of Independence fought from 1810 to 1820. But for the most part the Mexican Catholic Church was conservative and authoritarian, and worked to retain its high place in Mexican society.

Because the church was so often a repressive institution, the Mexican Revolution had a broad anticlerical (anti-Catholic) base. Revolutionary leaders regularly denounced the church and its influence over the Mexican people. Pancho Villa once said, "I do not deny belief in God. I affirm it and certify to it since it has comforted me and all men in many of life's crises. But I do not consider everything sacred that is covered by the name of religion. Most so called religious men use religion to promote their own interests."

Driven by ambition, Plutarco Elías Calles advanced as both a general and a politician. Always he tried to hook his star with Obregón. Both men were from the northern state of Sonora, but Calles lacked Obregón's charm and his sense of diplomacy. Obregón was a chief loved by many. Calles was a president feared by all. And Calles was never able to soften his rage against the Catholic Church.

In 1924, when Calles became president, the passions of the revolution were dwindling. The president then fanned the flames with his actions against the church. Calles supported a series of laws which forbade the teaching of religion in primary schools and which called for the deportation of foreign-born priests and nuns. The church reacted by going on strike. Priests refused to celebrate Sunday Mass or perform marriage and baptismal services. But Calles misread Mexican feelings for their church. To insult or disrespect the church is comparable to insulting a man's family. Such an insult demands a fight.

Tension between church and government triggered the short-lived Cristero War which broke out in 1927. Shouting their battle cry "*Viva Cristo Rey!*" ("Long live Christ the King!") angry Catholics burned schools and government buildings and attacked officials. The rioters, called *Cristeros*, singled out teachers in public schools because they brought "anti-religious" messages to their classrooms. Calles appointed army generals who he knew to be violently anticlerical and ordered them to put down the revolt in any manner they saw fit. The result was slaughter on a horrible scale. The historian Ramón Eduardo Ruiz said of the Cristero War, "Before the uprising subsided, soldiers killed priests, raped nuns, and looted churches, while *Cristeros*, not to be outdone, tortured and killed 'atheistic' schoolteachers. Some eighty thousand Mexicans died in this holy war."

The Power and the Glory

The Cristero War of the late 1920s is little known outside of Mexico. However the war was central to the powerful novel, *The Power and the Glory*, written by British author Graham Greene and published in 1940. The story tells of an alcoholic Catholic priest, a "whiskey priest," who lives in an area of Mexico where the Catholic religion has been outlawed by an anticlerical governor. In dramatic terms, the book explains how the priest escapes zealous law officers who wish to put him in front of a firing squad. If the priest would renounce his faith he would be free of such persecution, but this he refuses to do. Though the whiskey priest considers himself to be a failure, he still clings to his church and his calling.

Calles's term as president expired in 1928. With Calles stepping down, Alvaro Obregón ran for a second term as president. The Constitution forbade the reelection of presidents, but Obregón claimed that as long as he did not seek a consecutive term he was allowed reelection. Once more the words of the Constitution of 1917 were overlooked.

Obregón, with no real opposition, won reelection by a huge majority. On July 17, 1928, days after the election, Âlvaro Obregón sat in a suburban Mexico City restaurant eating dinner with friends. A young man in the restaurant held a sketch board and asked the president-elect if he could draw his picture. Obregón nodded as if to say yes. Suddenly the artist pulled a pistol from his coat pocket, pointed it at Obregón's face, and fired several shots. Obregón was killed instantly.

The murderer was a twenty-six-year-old Catholic fanatic named José de Léon Toral who believed Obregón had dishonored his church. Therefore, in his mind, God had commanded him to kill the president-elect. Religious zealots emerged everywhere in Mexico after the Revolution and after the Cristero War. Toral was brought to trial and executed by firing squad. His last words, shouted out before his death, echoed the Cristero War: "*Viva Cristo Rey!*"

Madre Conchita

Toral claimed he was inspired to murder Obregón through his association with a charismatic Catholic nun popularly called Madre Conchita. She was said to have a personality so powerful she readily took over the minds and wills of her followers. The nun was arrested, brought to trial, convicted of conspiring to overthrow the government, and sentenced to thirty years in prison. Many Mexican Catholics regarded Madre Conchita as a martyr not a murderer. When she was released from jail in 1940 she was greeted at the prison gates by hundreds of people who hailed her as a heroine and believed she should be named a saint.

At one time the assassination of a leading figure such as Obregón would have touched off a new civil war, but by the late 1920s the nation was tired of violence. President Calles, who was still in charge of the country at the time of the murder, allowed new elections to be held and agreed to leave office. At least this is what it appeared he had done. In fact, ex-president Calles acted as the country's *Jefe Máximo*, real boss, and ruled from his elegant plantation outside Mexico City. Three men served two-year terms as president at Calles's favor: Emilio Portes Gil (1928-1930), Pascual Ortiz Rubio (1930-1932), and Abelardo Rodriguez (1932-1934). They were not the true powers in the country. Graffiti written on the outside wall of the president's house told the real story:

Here lives the president
but the boss
resides in the house across the way.

The Mexican press called the stooge presidents "straw men," meaning they were empty-headed individuals who did nothing but follow the orders issued by Calles. This method of one-man rule behind a series of shadow presidents brought stability to Mexico, but those Mexicans who sought true democratic reform were left bitterly disappointed.

In 1934 a new president, Lázaro Cárdenas, was inaugurated in Mexico City. At that point the laws had changed, giving the president a six-year term. Initially most observers regarded Cárdenas as another straw man and predicted he would also be a puppet to the all-powerful Plutarco Calles. But Lázaro Cárdenas fooled the experts. After assuming the office he rose to become what many historians consider the greatest Mexican president of the twentieth century.

Lázaro Cárdenas del Río was born in 1885 in the state of Michoacán to a working-class family. His father owned a small store with a pool hall in the back. His father died when Lazaro was sixteen years old, leaving him in charge of his seven younger brothers and sisters. Cárdenas left school and went to work to support the family. To overcome his lack of formal education, he became an enthusiastic reader and poured through any book that came his way. When he was a teenager the Mexican Revolution broke out. At first he served as a rifleman, but rose to the rank of general by the age of twenty-five. His immediate commander was General Plutarco Elías Calles, who regarded him as a trustworthy man who faithfully followed orders.

In 1928 President Calles made Cárdenas the governor of Michoacán. Despite the lofty words of the Constitution, this was a common practice in Mexico. Important leaders gave government offices to their friends and cronies. The country was a democracy in name only. Only one political party mattered. Elections were held, but they were usually rigged. A ruling class made up of landholders and wealthy factory owners determined who would become state governors, senators, or even the nation's president. At the head of the ruling class in the 1920s stood Plutarco Elías Calles.

Unlike most governors, Cárdenas did not use his office to enrich himself. He spent tax money to build roads and schools. In his youth

President Lázaro Cárdenas del Río circa 1934

Cárdenas aspired to be a schoolteacher, and now he promoted education with more vigor than any other governor in the country. Somehow Plutarco Calles, the *Jefe Máximo*, overlooked Cárdenas's progressive record as governor of Michoacán, but Calles certainly did not want a progressive to serve as president. He preferred another straw man who would obey orders and maintain the status quo.

Yet, even while campaigning for the presidency, Cárdenas demonstrated his independence. He traveled more than 16,000 miles to every corner of the country asking for votes much in the manner of a presidential candidate in the United States. In rural areas he made his way down dusty trails on the back of a horse or a mule. Cárdenas had a remarkable memory and a mind for details. He wrote letters to farmers months after visiting them, inquiring about small matters such as a sick cow or a broken plow blade.

In office Cárdenas addressed the problem of land ownership, an inflammatory issue as old as Mexico itself. Spanish conquerors came in the 1500s, evicted the Native Americans from the best land, and distributed it among themselves. Mexico became a country of a few large landholders who owned sprawling haciendas and thousands of rural poor people who owned tiny plots or who were landless and worked on the haciendas. The Mexican Revolution of 1910 was fought largely to redress the inequalities of land ownership. But despite ten years of suffering and death Mexico remained a nation where the choice land was owned by a few families while masses of rural people were landless.

Every postwar president, starting with Obregón, vowed to redistribute land in a fairer manner. Token moves were made and courts stripped away some hacienda holdings and gave excess lands to collective farms called ejidos. Still no real progress was made as the hacienda owners (hacendados) had vast influence over government leaders and judges.

Then Lázaro Cárdenas became president. By the end of his term Cárdenas broke up large haciendas and gave 45 million acres to small farmers and to the ejidos. This figure is double the acreage redistributed by all the previous post-Revolution presidents put together.

Cárdenas made it a policy to reach out to small farmers, urging them to direct their grievances to his office. The president ordered the national telegraph service to provide free time one hour a day so farmers in the remote regions could send messages to his headquarters in Mexico City. It was said the waiting room adjoining Cárdenas' office told an interesting story: The men and women who were barefoot or who wore country-style sandals were seen first; those with stylish, highly-polished shoes waited.

Cárdenas embraced labor unions, another neglected element of Mexican society. Mexico at the time was a largely rural country with few industries. The unions that existed were weak. When labor strikes broke out the business owners who were affected called on the authorities—the police or the army—and the strikes were broken up, often with the use of clubs. These practices changed under Cárdenas. The president sent emissaries to try to settle the workplace problems. Labor mediators were instructed to listen carefully to both sides of a dispute before rendering an opinion.

Political enemies called President Cárdenas a socialist and even a communist. Cárdenas ruled in the 1930s when the Great Depression gripped the world and stagnated industrial economies. Socialism and communism appealed to working-class people who suffered from unemployment and distressing poverty. Cárdenas was not a communist, but the charges alone alarmed many leaders including the *Jefe Máximo*, Plutarco Elías Calles.

In 1936 loyal army officers reported to President Cárdenas that a group of rival officers were plotting to take over the government. The officers claimed that ex-president Calles was the secret leader of the plot. At about midnight on April 11, 1936, high-ranking soldiers banged on the door of Calles's country estate. Calles was told to pack a suitcase immediately and board an airplane waiting to take him to exile in the United States. Hours later the plane landed in Dallas, Texas, where Calles told reporters, "I was expelled from Mexico for fighting communism."

Calles used communism as a scare word, perhaps hoping to goad U.S. leaders into disposing of the Mexican president. This did not happen. Years earlier U.S. President Franklin Roosevelt proclaimed the "Good Neighbor" policy which curtailed the practice of U.S. interference in the domestic affairs of its neighbors to the south. Calles stayed in the United States until Mexican leaders allowed him to return to Mexico in 1942, and lived quietly in Mexico City until his death in 1945. A few months before his death, Calles, who led Mexico into the anti-Catholic Cristero War, claimed he had acquired a belief in God.

The Revolution had ruined Mexico's economy, and recovery was slow. Factories were closed, farmers' fields empty of crops, and the railroad system—once the pride of Mexico—barely functioned. But one industry, oil, still thrived. Oil virtually bubbled out of the soil along Mexico's Gulf Coast. The Aztecs burned oil in their ceremonies, and the Spaniards used it to caulk their ships. The first commercial oil well opened in 1901, and for a brief spell in 1921 Mexico was the world's largest oil producer.

In the 1930s Mexico remained a major oil exporter, but the nation's largest oil fields were owned by U.S. and British companies. Foreign ownership of the oil industry had begun during the Díaz years. The arrangement always angered Mexican nationalists who believed their country should own and operate all its sub surface resources.

After a series of violent labor strikes President Cárdenas nationalized the oil industry on March of 1938. It was a bold, dramatic, and even dangerous move. With the signing of one document the president claimed Mexican oil was now owned by the national government. The action conformed with the 1917 Constitution which

President Cárdenas announces the nationalization of
foreign oil companies on March 18, 1938.

stated that all the country's natural resources belonged to the Mexican people and cannot be exploited by outsiders.

Oil companies in the United States and Great Britain were enraged by the takeover of the oil fields. Some corporate leaders in the United States urged President Roosevelt to send the Marines into Mexico and retake the petroleum companies' properties. Mexican politicians, in turn, suggested that Cárdenas blow up the oil fields to thwart such an invasion. Cooler heads won the day. Roosevelt's Good Neighbor policy prevailed, and there was no U.S. invasion of its southern neighbor.

The people of Mexico rejoiced at Cárdenas's takeover of the oil fields. Shortly after the president made the announcement cheering crowds gathered at the great plaza in downtown Mexico City, the Zocalo, and began shouting "Mexico for the Mexicans!" Men and women started a spontaneous parade that wound through the streets of the capital for six hours. Earlier Cárdenas had made a radio speech asking for donations to tide the government over until money could be earned from the newly nationalized oil industry. That night Mexicans gave generously to collection boxes put up in the Zocalo. The rich gave golden watches and rings; the poor donated eggs and live chickens. Someone wrote a folk ballad, a *corrido*, that was sung on the street:

> On the eighteen of March, the day of the great sensation!
> He nationalized the oil then! The Chief of our Nation . . .
> And so Mexico is giving the world its great lesson!
> History is being redeemed through our Revolution . . .

National Holiday

March 18 is still a national holiday, *La Expropiación Petrolera* (the Appropriation of Oil), and is celebrated in Mexico with parades and patriotic speeches.

Cárdenas left office when his presidential term expired in 1940, a tense year for the world. A shooting war raged in Europe, and even more war loomed in the Pacific. But Mexico enjoyed peace, thanks largely to the leadership of Lázaro Cárdenas. He took over a country still feeling the pain of civil war and brought it to stability. The Revolution shaped modern Mexico, and Cárdenas is often called "the moral conscience of the Revolution."

A mural of Miguel Hidalgo y Costilla by painter José Clemente Orozco. The mural is in the stairwell of the Jalisco governmental palace in Guadalajara, Mexico.

CHAPTER 3

An Explosion in the Arts

The philosopher and poet Octavio Paz said of the Mexican Revolution, "It is the Revolution, the magical word, the word that is going to change everything . . . The Revolution was a sudden immersion of Mexico in her own being, from which she brought back up, almost blindly, the essentials of a new kind of state . . . Therefore it was also a fiesta: 'the fiesta of bullets.'" This "fiesta" liberated Mexican thought and inspired another revolution in the arts and in literature. But before a cultural revolution could properly begin, Mexican leaders had to address a problem that had plagued the nation for centuries: illiteracy.

In the past the Catholic church was largely responsible for running Mexico's school system. Priests taught classes, but they often concentrated on having their students memorize prayers rather than teaching them basic reading and arithmetic. Also, the church charged tuition so only rich and middle-class families were able to send their children to the Catholic schools. Because the country had no effective public school system, illiteracy was widespread. By 1910, only 15 percent of the Mexican people could read and write.

Then came the Revolution and the Constitution of 1917. Language in the Constitution guaranteed every Mexican child a free education, paid for by public funds. When the shooting war finally ended President Alvaro Obregón made educating his nation a primary goal.

In 1921 Obregón appointed José Vasconcelos to be secretary of public education. It proved to be a brilliant choice. Vasconcelos was already famous as a philosopher and historian. He believed that Mexico and other Latin American peoples must form their own philosophical traditions, free from European or United States influences. His philosophy of *indigenismo* promoted the contributions of Native Americans in all the Latin American republics. He called mestizos *La Raza Cósmica* (The Cosmic Race).

As head of public education Vasconcelos went about his work as if he had declared war against illiteracy. His administration built one thousand schools, many in rural areas where schools never existed before. Government-owned printing houses churned out textbooks and delivered them, sometimes on the backs of mules, to the far-flung country schools where even roads did not exist. Under his direction funding for the school system exceeded that of the military for the first time in Mexican history.

Vasconcelos regularly spoke before graduating classes at teachers' colleges. He gave fiery talks which sent young teachers marching to the school systems with the determination of soldiers entering battle. Not satisfied with confining education to the classroom, Vasconcelos sponsored a program that encouraged school children to teach their parents how to read. These at-home lessons were carried out by candlelight in thousands of dirt-floor peasant huts where ten year olds, fresh from the classrooms, pointed word for word at a book and brought the magic of reading to their parents. In Vasconcelos's first four years in office, illiteracy in Mexico declined by 30 percent.

Under President Obregón, José Vasconcelos also served as the nation's cultural chief. At his direction Mexico's National Symphonic Orchestra was established. Literature flourished as novelists and historians labored to explain the carnage of the Mexican Revolution.

A 1914 photo of José Vasconcelos

Talented writers and musicians were given small salaries paid by the government. Although they were being compensated with government funds, Vasconcelos insisted they be free to compose what they wished.

It was in the field of art that Mexicans thrilled the world. Mexican painters looked to their nation's past as fountains for inspiration. Murals were an early Mexican art form. Paintings decorated the inside walls of temples built by the Olmecs, the Mayas, the Aztecs, and other ancient Mexican societies. When the Spaniards came, priests directed Indian artists to paint the walls of churches with scenes that told biblical stories to people who could not read the Bible. The European priests were astonished with the skills shown by native Mexican painters. Some priests even suggested that the Indians must be aided by the devil who mysteriously guided their hands.

After the Revolution the muralists of Mexico began to write their own chapter in art history. Throughout the world, the early twentieth century was an exciting age in artistic expression. Impressionism, pioneered largely by the French, allowed artists to blend form with light and create a sense of movement on canvasses. Cubism, fostered by the Spanish, urged painters to study a subject from several viewpoints and to render contrasting and even surrealistic works of art. Mexicans took wall paintings to their highest form and created what is called the Mexican Mural Renaissance.

Murals painted in Mexico stood as public art, works to be enjoyed by the masses. The 1920s and 1930s were thrilling decades because average Mexicans came to realize the wonderful paintings decorating their public buildings were being rendered for their enjoyment. Also, all knew their painters were capturing the attention of art lovers throughout the world. Mexico rose as an art-happy country whose people worshiped their muralists as super heroes. Three major painters—Diego Rivera, David Alfaro Siqueiros, and Jose Clemente Orozco—led the Mexican Mural Renaissance. These men were the "Big Three," and they captured the adoration of their countrymen.

Dr. Atl

Mexico's master muralists had a master teacher in Dr. Atl. He was born Geraldo Murillo in the city of Guadalajara in 1875 and changed his name to Dr. Atl (*atl* was an Aztec word for "water") when he was a young painter. Dr. Atl traveled in Europe studying art and rendering magnificent paintings, often of outdoor scenes. He was a student and later a teacher at the Academy of San Carlos in Mexico City. From this post he befriended Mexican artists, including Diego Rivera, and exercised a profound influence over the Mexican muralist movement.

The tomb of Dr. Atl at the Panteon Civil de Dolores cemetery in Mexico City

Of the Big Three, Diego Rivera attracted the most attention. He was a large man, weighing more than three hundred pounds. Usually he dressed in an unkempt manner, wearing a cloak splashed with spots of paint. Rivera was an outspoken communist and an atheist, and he frequently put political and anti-religious messages into his artwork. He viewed murals as a high form of public art, a vehicle for education as well as enjoyment. True art, he believed, should not be confined to works on canvass which are displayed in living rooms and viewed only by a private audience. He once wrote, "The painter who does not feel attuned to the aspirations of the masses—this man may not produce a work of permanent worth. Not so the man who paints walls [of] public buildings. Art cut off from practical aims is not art."

Diego Rivera was born in1886 in Guanajuato, a hill town in central Mexico. The town is a maze of twisting narrow streets, and an almost constant sun blazes above its tiled rooftops. Perhaps the light and natural color of Guanajuato compelled Rivera to become an artist. He said, "As far back as I can remember, I was drawing. Almost as soon as my fat baby fingers could grasp a pencil, I was marking up walls doors and furniture. To avoid mutilation of his entire house, my father set aside a special room where I was allowed to write on anything I wished."

Rivera's father was a minor town official, a position that gave him respect but little cash. When Diego was five the family moved to Mexico City where the father could earn more money. The capital in the 1890s was a fascinating place for a curious boy like Diego Rivera. Electric lights shined in the streets after dark. Buildings along the broad Zocalo contained all the chapters of Mexican history. The city was too exciting for the boy and he began skipping school and exploring the sprawling neighborhoods. Of course he saw brutal poverty. This was during the Porfirio Díaz years when country people who lost their farms to the large haciendas streamed into the capital looking for work. The plight of the poor jarred his thinking and perhaps led him to believe communism offered a better way of life than free enterprise as it was practiced in Mexico.

When not wandering the capital's streets, young Rivera lost himself in drawing. He sketched people, trees, buildings, and even his visions of great battles in history. Professors at the Academy of San Carlos, a leading Mexico City art school, must have been impressed with his drawings for they allowed him to enroll at the age of ten. As was true with almost all Mexican institutions the academy taught art through European principals. Diego and the other students were required to copy Spanish master painters. Rivera devoted himself to the work. As a teenager he won several scholarship grants enabling him to travel to Europe to further his studies.

In Paris, his favorite city in Europe, Rivera was a hit in the sidewalk cafes because he was witty and charming as well as being an enormously talented painter. Cafe society regarded him as exotic, an untamed man from a wild country that was at the time tearing itself apart in civil war. Before World War I broke out, the Mexican Revolution captivated

Diego Rivera, 1932

Europeans who viewed it as a contest between good and evil: "good" were the rebellious peasants, "evil" the greedy landowners. Rivera boosted his image by claiming to be a warrior who had fought side-by-side with General Emiliano Zapata. Actually Rivera lived and worked in Europe from 1907 to 1921, thus spending all the revolutionary war years away from home. Storytelling was one of Rivera's many gifts. He held Europeans rapt with far-fetched tales of a made-up soldier's life during the Revolution.

When Rivera returned to Mexico he befriended José Vasconselos who gave him a prime commission: he was to direct a mural painted on the inside walls of the newly completed Ministry of Education building in downtown Mexico City. It was a perfect project for Diego Rivera. He was a tireless worker (to him a fourteen-hour workday was routine) and a zealous believer in the worth of public art. He and his assistants built scaffolds and threw themselves into the task of bringing the walls of the education headquarters building to life. Often it was frustrating work, requiring the artist to rework every detail over and over again. Late one evening one of his assistants walked the halls and noticed, "that the painter's scaffold was trembling as if at the start of an earthquake. Coming near, I saw Rivera's dim bulk at the top. Climbing to investigate, I found him crying and viciously picking off his day's job with a small trowel as a child will kick down a sand castle in a tantrum."

For three years Rivera and his team labored on the Ministry of Education building. Today the murals they created stand as a masterpiece of the era. The work consists of 124 panels painted on each of the building's three floors. The vast wall paintings present Mexican life with an emphasis on men and women at work. One of the most dramatic scenes is called *Entering The Mine*. It shows mine workers, picks and shovels on their shoulders, plodding into the mouth of a mine. Conditions in the silver mines in Rivera's native state of Guanajuato were brutal for workers, and the artist captured the laborers' pain. The men file into the mine ponderously, reluctantly, as if they were entering the jaws of hell.

Mexican Influence on U. S. Public Art

The United States, along with the rest of the world, suffered through the Great Depression in the 1930s. In order to promote employment, the administration of President Franklin Roosevelt established the Works Project Administration (WPA) which gave work to people in many fields, including the arts. One of the tasks given to WPA artists was to create murals on public buildings. To do this the WPA painters studied the superb public art being created in Mexico. In this manner, the fame of the Mexican Mural Renaissance spread to the United States and beyond.

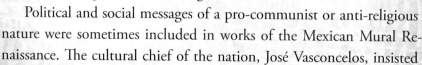

Rivera's most well-known mural was painted at the National Palace, which rises over the Zocalo in Mexico City. The building and its wall art is seen by thousands of people every day as it is a focal point for groups of foreign tourists and for school classes led by teachers. The National Palace mural, called *The Epic of the Mexican People*, traces Mexican history back to pre-Columbian times (before the coming of the Spaniards). The pictures are brilliant and colorful, but—critics claim—they are heavy-handed with Rivera's personal interpretations of past events. The Aztecs are seen as a nature-loving people who built a monumental civilization in central Mexico. There is no mention that the Aztecs practiced human sacrifice on a grizzly scale and that they waged aggressive wars on their neighbors. Spaniards arrive and Rivera shows them enslaving and torturing Aztec men and women. The true devil in the mural is the Spanish leader, Hernan Cortés, who is pictured as a hideous-looking man seen selling Aztec slaves for gold.

Political and social messages of a pro-communist or anti-religious nature were sometimes included in works of the Mexican Mural Renaissance. The cultural chief of the nation, José Vasconcelos, insisted

The History of Mexico, a mural by Diego Rivera, created from 1929 to 1935, located in the National Palace in Mexico City

the artists have freedom of expression. So he simply looked the other way when they injected controversial themes into their art. Large segments of the Mexican public strongly disagreed with the opinions of certain artists. Public art in the 1920s and 1930s was taken seriously, indeed, passionately by the Mexican people. The murals were theirs, as if they were being painted on the walls of their living rooms. Therefore the people reacted, sometimes violently, to the murals' content. In Mexico City crowds threw rocks at the muralists whose paintings they thought were offensive. Art students got into ragging arguments and even fistfights with those who dared find fault with the master muralists. The debates grew so intense that Rivera painted murals with a pistol in his pocket to use if he had to defend himself from an upset viewer.

Few Mexicans had complaints against one of the Big Three artists, José Clemente Orozco, because he shunned controversial messages. Orozco was suspicious of all political movements, including communism. In fact, though he was known as "the painter of the Revolution," he was critical even of that chapter in history. When he did depict the 1910-1920 war he portrayed the horrors of warfare, never its assumed glory. The war, he believed, had hurt the nation's poor. In one painting Orozco shows a drunken revolutionary general holding up a prize of war: a laced stocking off the leg of a prostitute. Orozco, who tended to be moody and sullen, preferred to paint scenes of gaiety. His favorite subjects were men and women out for the evening, dancing, drinking, dining, and trying to enjoy life.

David Alfaro Siqueiros was an avowed communist and was even more devoted to the cause than Rivera. He grew up in the state of Chihuahua, the son of a Catholic and very wealthy family. From a young age he asked why he should live in luxury when surrounded by families struggling to put a few tortillas on the table. He came to believe communism was a just and logical future for Mexico and for the world. He dedicated his life to communism and to public art. Siqueiros founded the Syndicate of Painters and Sculptors and wrote its charter which urged artists, "to produce only monumental work for the public domain . . . a rich art for the people instead of an expression of individual pleasure." Experts agreed that as an artist he was superb. Siqueiros was the youngest of the Big Three and he readily accepted new techniques such as using spray paint guns on murals. David Alfaro Siqueiros created many profound murals, when he was not in jail or hiding from the law. He served several long terms in prison for communist or radical activities.

José Vasconcelos remained the nation's cultural leader and was loosely in charge of the muralists throughout the Obregón years. He resigned as secretary of public education in 1924 when Calles became president. Vasconcelos believed the Calles presidency was a step backwards to the days of dictatorship before the Revolution. In 1929 Vasconcelos ran for president. He was defeated by Pascual Ortiz Rubio, one of Calles's notorious "straw men." Vasconcelos claimed the vote count was fraudulent and that Calles and his followers stole the election. He remained bitter over his presidential defeat for the rest of his life.

Women and the Vote

One of the campaign promises Vasconcelos made was to extend voting privileges to women for the first time in Mexican history. The issue of women's suffrage was defeated with him. Women did not win the right to vote in Mexico until 1953.

Literature flourished in the 1920s and 1930s, but Mexican writers did not achieve the international fame enjoyed by the artists. For the most part Mexican novels and poetry were read at home. This gave writers a limited audience since the Mexican reading public was still small.

Marian Azuela was the most notable writer of the post-revolutionary war era. He served as a doctor in the army of Pancho Villa. In his book *Los de Abaho* (usually translated as *The Underdogs*) he addresses the confusion of the Revolution. Toward the end of the conflict few common soldiers understood the causes for which they were fighting. In the last chapter Azuela portrays his main character, Demetrio, leading his troops into still another one of the war's endless and seemingly pointless battles:

> A curse breaks from Demitrio's parched throat.
> "Fire at 'em. Shoot any man who runs away!
> "Storm the hill!" he roars like a wild beast.
> But the enemy, lying in ambush by the thousand, open up their machine gun fire and Demetrio's men fall like wheat under the sickle . . ."

Throughout the post-revolutionary era muralists were worshiped as heroes. Their comings and goings were reported in the press in the manner that movie stars or baseball greats were covered in a later era. Of the muralists, Diego Rivera continued to be the most flamboyant and drew the greatest attention. His women companions were always hot topics in the newspapers and among the rumor mills. Rivera was never satisfied with having just one girlfriend or even one wife. In turn, women found him to be almost magnetically irresistible. Big, bulging eyes, wildly uncombed hair, he once described himself as being, "attractively ugly." Many of his women friends stayed by his side while grudgingly accepting his desires to have other female companions in his life. One woman broke this pattern and demanded his loyalty.

Frida Kahlo was born in 1907 in Mexico City to a German immigrant father and a Mexican mother. As a child she showed exceptional talent as a painter, but decided to study medicine. At age eighteen she rode on a Mexico City bus when it collided with a streetcar, driving an iron pole through her body as if the pole were a spear. After many operations she recovered but suffered terrible bouts of pain for the rest of her life. Even before the accident, Frida had met Diego Rivera. He was charmed by her intelligence, her creativity, and especially her artistic abilities.

The Two Fridas

One of Frida Kahlo's most intriguing paintings is *Los Dos Fridas* (*The Two Fridas*), completed in 1939. It is a twin self-portrait showing the traditional Mexican woman (Frida in the white dress) contrasted by the stronger modern woman (Frida in the darker dress). The hearts of both women are exposed. The more traditional Frida's heart is wounded and dripping blood. The work is believed to be an allegory of Frida Kahlo's constant struggles as she endured bouts of physical and emotional pain shadowed by her inner strength.

Frida Kahlo enjoyed painting in bright colors and using her imagination to create scenes which surprised viewers and set them to wondering. Diego Rivera and Frida Kahlo married in 1929. It was a union of opposites. He weighted a spongy three hundred pounds; she a slight one hundred. At the time of their marriage Diego was forty-two years old and Frida twenty-one. They fought often—in public in Mexico City night clubs and privately at home. Most often they clashed over Diego's infidelity. Details of their battles were reported by the scandal-loving Mexico City press. They divorced, then remarried, and still they fought.

Cardenas and the Exiles

Leon Trotsky entered Mexico through a program instituted in the late 1930s by President Lázaro Cárdenas. The program encouraged political exiles from around the world to come to Mexico and gain citizenship. Cardenas reasoned that many exiles were educated professionals—doctors, business people, and teachers—whose presence would help Mexico progress. For the most part, the policy worked well. A civil war was being fought in Spain during the late 1930s, and Mexico gained many useful residents who fled the fighting.

Leon Trotsky

The two agreed on one subject: both were communists. In the late 1930s they invited the exiled leader of communist Russia, Leon Trotsky, to live with them in their Mexico City home. At first all were happy. Trotsky and Rivera stayed up late night after night discussing how communism would spread and change the world. But soon Trotsky had a brief affair with Frida Kahlo. The encounter enraged Diego Rivera, even though he chronically cheated on his wife. Diego Rivera ended his friendship with Trotsky and ordered the Russian out of his house.

In 1940, Trotsky was assassinated in Mexico City by an agent of the Russian strongman, Joseph Stalin. The killing was a particularly

Frida Kahlo and Diego Rivera in 1932

gory affair as the assassin struck Trotsky on the head with an axe. The murder dominated national news for months afterward. The story had everything: blood, sex, international intrigue, and it involved the two icons of Mexican society—Frida Kahlo and Diego Rivera. The Trotsky assassination had no lasting impact on Mexican history, but the sensation it caused pointed out that in Mexico artists had risen to the status of superstars.

An 1849 map of the U.S. and Mexico drawn by George W. Colton

CHAPTER 4

Closer Neighbors

The United States and Mexico border stretches some 2,000 miles. In the east the border is defined by the Rio Grande River. To the west there is no distinct boundary and only signs and barbed wire fences separate the two nations. The United States is the richest country in the world; Mexico one of the poorest. No where else in the world does a single border separate an impoverished country from a rich state and a superpower. Geographically they are close, but life on opposite sides of their borders is radically different. A modern author called the two nations "Distant Neighbors."

Up to the 1940s the people of both countries generally held a negative view of each other. Americans saw Mexico as a lawless state where civil war was constant and where rampaging bandits terrorized travelers. Mexicans, especially the intellectuals, looked upon America as a bullying power whose army had invaded

Mexico in the past and whose greedy corporations owned factories and mines in Mexico and exploited the workers. Gradually the bitterness and the mistrust between the neighbors lessened. Tourism, trade, cultural exchange, and the pressures of war helped to reduce suspicions and promote friendship.

United States Interventions Into Mexico

Three times in the past the U. S. military crossed the southern border and invaded Mexican territory. In the Mexican-American War of 1846-1848 the United States acquired its southwestern states and California from Mexico; in 1914 U.S. forces seized the port city of Veracruz; in 1916 U.S. calvary troops entered northern Mexico in pursuit of Pancho Villa who had raided the town of Columbus, New Mexico.

Year by year the passion of the Revolution faded and a time of political maturity in Mexico began. Manual Ávila Camacho was elected president of Mexico in 1940. Ávila Camacho was a soldier during the Revolution, but he was too young to be an important commander. Under Ávila Camacho's presidency the influence of the army diminished. "I belong to the army, and I love it very much," he declared. "But for Mexico the era of the generals is over now. I am sure that civilians will successfully do their duty."

Ávila Camacho also ended the conflict between church and state with a single statement: "I am a Catholic by origin, [and] in moral feeling." No prior president since the Revolution or the bloody Cristero War had acknowledged following any religion, much less Catholicism. Mexicans, most of whom were Catholics, hailed the new relationship between their church and their government. To this day church and state remain strictly separate institutions, but since Ávila Camacho the two are no longer at odds with each other.

Following the lead of José Vasconcelos, a new nationwide literacy program was launched. A law was passed that required anyone who knew how to read to teach literacy to those who could not read. The law provided for penalties and fines for people refusing to teach or refusing to learn, but rarely did such fines have to be applied. They gladly complied with the literacy law. Thus middle-class housewives taught their maids how to read while bankers taught their janitors.

Mexico at the time of Ávila Camacho was not a true democracy. Mexican presidents were selected by an inner circle of government officials led by the ex-president. The process was called *el dedazo* (the pointing finger). This method began under Obregón who pointed his finger at Calles and said, in effect, "You're the next president." Calles, in turn, selected his three "straw men" and then named Cárdenas president in a decision he later regretted. Cárdenas, the most democratic-minded of Mexico's leaders, made Ávila Camacho his successor in the finger-pointing manner.

All these chiefs of state ran in presidential elections and campaigned for votes as if the final result was in doubt. But it was the before-election process, the *el dedazo*, that really mattered. Once a president was selected by a closed-door, finger-pointing group the voters were presented with only one viable candidate. The man named by the pointing finger always won the general election. Voters were asked only to confirm an established fact. Commenting on this system the American political scientist Frank Brandenberg said, "Mexicans avoid personal dictatorships by retiring their dictators every six years."

In 1946 the *Partido Revolucionario Institucional* (the Party of Revolutionary Institutions, usually referred to by its initials PRI) was established. The PRI was simply a name-change given to an older political party that emerged after the Revolution. With the PRI the finger-pointing method of presidential selection was formalized. Mexico became essentially a one-party state. Through the rest of the twentieth century the PRI never lost a presidential election or a contest of state governors.

On December 7, 1941, Japanese aircraft bombed Pearl Harbor, plunging the United States into World War II. Mexico faced three alternatives: the country could aid the United States, it could favor the Axis powers of Germany and Japan, or it could stay neutral. The thought of supporting the Japanese warlords and the Nazis in Germany was abhorrent in Mexico. Hopes of neutrality were dashed when a German submarine sank a tanker in Mexican waters. Mexico entered the war on the side of the United States and Great Britain in May 1942. It marked the first time Mexico had ever engaged in a war beyond its borders.

After the Japanese bombing of Pearl Harbor, a burned B-17C aircraft rests near Hangar Number Five at Hickam Field in Oahu, Hawaii.

Relations with the United States warmed during World War II. In April 1943 President Franklin Roosevelt and President Ávila Camacho met in the northern Mexican city of Monterrey. It was the first time a sitting American president visited Mexico. The two heads of state made trade agreements that kept vital oil and other raw materials flowing from Mexico to industries in the U.S. Mexico also agreed to furnish an air force unit to the war effort. Flying P-47 Thunderbolt fighters, the Mexican pilots participated in the invasion of the Philippines where they fought bravely and became heroes at home. The unit, Squadron 201, was called the "Aztec Eagles" because the ancient Aztecs worshiped the graceful eagle.

Mexican movies bloomed during the war years. Unlike the work of the muralists the films were not successful in the United States, but the rest of Latin America hailed Mexicans as genius movie-makers. The period of 1935 through the 1950s is called The Golden Age of Mexican Cinema. An early Golden Age film was the historical epic *Vamanos con Pancho Villa!* (1935), which broke a long-standing pattern and portrayed Pancho Villa's cruelty instead of his heroism. The movie *La Perla* (*The Pearl*), released in 1945, is set in a fishing village and tells of an impoverished couple's frantic efforts to find medical treatment for their young son who has been bitten by a deadly scorpion. *La Perla*, with its script written by the American novelist John Steinbeck, won several international awards.

Of the Golden Age movie stars, the comic actor Cantinflas was the most beloved. He was born Mario Moreno in Mexico City in 1911. As a youth he made up the name Cantinflas and used it to hide the fact that he was secretly performing in neighborhood theaters. His parents believed acting was an ignoble profession. Cantinflas frequently played a poorly educated country man trying to build a new life in a big city. The character caught on because at the time many country families had moved to cities and were making the adjustment to urban life. In his movies Cantinflas is polite and smiling, but secretly he is a trouble-maker as he works to improve the lives of his impoverished neighbors.

He first appeared in a movie in 1940. Before that he tried to earn a living as a professional boxer. His moves in the ring were so comical they made the audience—and his opponent—laugh. So, Cantinflas gave up boxing to become Mexico's greatest comedian.

"Los Olvidados"

One of Mexico's classic films made in the Golden Age is *Los Olvidados* (*The Forgotten Ones*), released in 1950. It is a grim story, telling the plight of a gang of homeless boys living on the streets of Mexico City. The boys will do anything to survive. In one scene they beat up and rob a blind street musician. Though telling a gloomy tale, the director freely slips into fantasy by exploring the boys' dreams. *Los Olvidadeos*, often translated into English as *The Young and the Damned*, won the Best Director award at the Cannes Film Festival of 1951. Today historians and critics praise the film as a gem of Mexico's Golden Age of Cinema.

A scene from *Los Olvidados*

Mexican music crossed the northern border and charmed Americans. During the busy wartime years Americans found themselves whistling, humming, or trying to sing the words of "*Allá en el Rancho Grande*." The peppy song depicting the Mexican farm country was heard on American radios and became a hit:

> *Allá en el Rancho Grande*
>
> Out there on the Big Ranch
>
> *Allá donde vivía . . . .*
>
> Out there where I used to Live . . . .

Another popular song of the 1940s was "South of the Border" (Down Mexico Way), a ballad, written by an American, that tells of a cowboy in love with a Mexican señorita. Music is said to be "the international language," and through music understanding and friendship grew between the distant neighbors.

For the average Mexican the wartime program called *El Bracero* was the most important measure of the era. The Spanish word *bracero* simply means "arm," but in the U.S. it was interpreted as the "helping hand." Mexican farm workers, *braceros*, were given temporary papers and free transportation to come north of the border and help bring in harvests. The policy benefited both countries. In the United States during World War II people left the farms to take high paying factory jobs in the cities. Mexicans replaced the farm workers and earned far more money than they could at home. Some 300,000 Mexicans joined the *Bracero* program and experienced life in the prosperous United States for the first time. Upon returning, they told others how well working-class Americans lived in comparison to Mexican workers. In the near future dreams of life in *El Norte* ("The North," a popular term for the United States) would grip millions of Mexicans.

In 1946 Miguel Alemán became Mexico's president. Alemán was born in the state of Veracruz in 1902. His father was a powerful army general during the Revolution. As a young man, Alemán moved to Mexico City where he became a successful lawyer and rose in the ranks of the PRI.

Mexican presidents, the good ones as well as the mediocre ones, are always history-makers because the Constitution of 1917 gives the president extraordinary powers. In the United States the president can be overruled by the congress or the court system. In Europe the legislative branch of government can have greater power than the chief executive. This is not true in Mexico, where the president rules with almost absolute authority.

Writers of the 1917 Constitution wished to promote stability. Since gaining independence from Spain in 1820, Mexico suffered through a series of civil wars, interrupted only by the thirty-year-long dictator-ship of Porfirio Díaz. In order to change this pattern the creators of the Constitution heaped powers on the chief executive and made Mexico a presidential democracy rather than a parliamentary democracy, as is common in today's Europe. Each president is given a *sextino*, a six-year period where he can govern the country almost as absolutely as an Old World monarch. In terms of establishing stability, the Constitution has served the nation well. There have been no civil wars for almost one hundred years.

Presidents of Mexico (1920-1952)

Alvaro Obregón (1920-1924)

Plutarco Elias Calles (1924-1928)

Emilio Potes Gil (1928-1930)

Pascual Ortiz Rubio (1930-1932)

Abelardo L. Rodriguez (1932-1934)

Lázaro Cárdenas (1934-1940)

Manual Ávila Camacho (1940-1946)

Miguel Alemán (1946-1952)

Miguel Alemán was more a businessman than he was a politician. He once declared, "what was good for business was good for Mexico." The new president altered the course of post-revolutionary Mexico by promoting business and industry and favoring institutions in the cities. The Revolution was largely a war of farmers battling for land. When he campaigned for office, Alemán praised the peasant soldiers and the agrarian spirit of the war. Usually he was accompanied by lesser of-fice-seekers, called *jilgueros* (songbirds,) who also extolled the farmer/soldiers and Mexico's agricultural heritage. Once in office, however, Alemán concentrated on building factories and hotels in the cities, and he turned an indifferent eye on the problems of small farmers.

Miguel Alemán

Encouraging tourism became the new president's prime goal. Tourism brought foreign currency, usually U.S. dollars, into the Mexican economy. Under Alemán's leadership tourism soon provided more jobs than any other single industry. Well-to-do Americans began making Mexico their special vacationland during the World War II years. The rich wanted an exotic place to travel. Europe was denied to them because of the war, and therefore the country next door served as a welcome alternative. Hotels catering to wealthy visitors sprouted up in Mexico City. Elegant restaurants were built, lining the capital city's boulevards. The hotels and restaurants employed thousands of city-dwellers, but the sudden emphasis on tourism defied the rural and egalitarian ideals of the Revolution. This wartime shift in economic priorities turned a new chapter in Mexican history. Octavio Paz noted, "It was during the Second World War that the actual revolutionary period of modern Mexico came to an end and the period of economic development began."

Of all Mexican destinations, Acapulco loomed highest in the tourists' dreams. Once a sleepy port city on the Pacific, Acapulco rose as a resort famous for its silvery beaches, constant sun, and gentle waters. Hollywood led the parade to Acapulco. American movie stars such as Frank Sinatra, Elizabeth Taylor, John Wayne, and Johnny "Tarzan" Weismuller established second homes in the city. President Alemán completed the parade by constructing the nation's finest highway connecting Mexico City and Acapulco. The highway ended at a broad boulevard appropriately named *Costera Miguel Alemán* which swept around Acapulco Bay and gave motorists stunning vistas.

In addition to tourism, Alemán encouraged industrial growth in the classic manner: he kept taxes low and labor unions weak. This too was in violation of revolutionary principals which extolled a triumph of the poor over the power of the rich. To Alemán labor unions were somewhat of a nuisance. He had to compliment labor in his speeches or risk upsetting his place in post-revolutionary Mexico. But he believed strikes weakened business and scared investors. Mexican labor practices were ruled by draconian laws which could be interpreted many ways by judges friendly with the president. "There must be no illegal work stoppages," Alemán said upon taking office. As president, he—and usually he alone—determined just what constituted an "illegal work stoppage."

With Alemán's blessings foreign investment flowed into Mexico. This practice too ran contrary to the lessons of the Revolution. Under the dictatorship of Porfirio Díaz foreign companies came to own many key Mexican industries. A spirited battle cry shouted out during the war was, "Mexico for the Mexicans!" Now many accused Alemán of selling out Mexico once more. The president responded by claiming the nation needed foreign investment money to grow the economy. As Alemán wished, dollars and new goods entered the economy. Kellogg's Corn Flakes and Rice Krispies, made and packaged by factories in Mexico, appeared on grocery shelves and stood alongside cans of Campbell's soup. Newly built factories owned by the American companies Ford and Chrysler churned out auto parts. In 1950, some 63,500 factories operated in Mexico, an increase of about 20,000 industrial plants over 1940.

South of the capital a gleaming university complex was built on what was a barren lava field. The new campus housed the National Autonomous University of Mexico (UNAM) which had previously occupied a few scattered buildings in Mexico City. This *Ciudad Universitaria* (University City) showcased another Mexican art form: architecture. Spreading over 550 acres the UNAM buildings were designed by 150 of the nation's best architects and engineers. When completed in 1954, the University City represented modern architecture with a distinctive Mexican slant. The outside walls of the library were covered with a mosaic, designed by Juan O' Gorman, and representing Mexican cultural history dating to pre-Columbian times. A focal point was the fifteen-story administration building which, significantly, stood next to an oversized statue of Miguel Alemán.

The Latin American Tower

Pride of the Alemán-inspired building boom was the Latin American Tower, which opened in 1956. Rising forty-five stories in the heart of Mexico City the building was for many years the tallest in Latin America and the fourth tallest in the world. It's construction was especially daunting because the high-rise had to be built to withstand Mexico City's all too frequent earthquakes.

The outside walls of the central library at the National Autonomous University of Mexico are covered by a mosaic designed by Juan O' Gorman in the early 1950s. The mosaic, which is recognized as the world's largest mural, represents Mexican culture and history dating back to pre-Columbian times.

In the years after World War II, the Mexican economy expanded by 6 to 7 seven percent a year, one of the highest growth rates of any nation on earth. While the economy enlarged, government money was channeled to build roads and other public projects. The free-flowing funds bred corruption, which became a sad legacy of the Alemán administration.

Official corruption in Mexico began under the Spaniards and lasted through the independence movement and the Revolution. Corruption was so widespread that people accepted it with a shrug of the shoulders and the words so commonly heard in the country, "*ni modo*," meaning "what can one do?" Leaders often collected money in the form of bribes called *morditas*, or "little bites." A highway-construction contractor, for example, had to pay a *mordita* to a politician before the politician would sign a building permit. Hard-working Mexicans loathed those who took *morditas*, but they recognized they could do little to end the practice.

Profiting from inside information was another road to riches for powerful politicians. Years after he left office, Ramón Beteta, the treasury secretary under Alemán, explained, "There are so many ways by which a functionary can enrich himself, and they are not strictly speaking illegal, although they are not ethical either. Consider, for example, the public official who knows that a new highway is about to open . . . [the official can] purchase, either directly or through intermediaries the properties along this highway and thus make a killing."

President Alemán was among those who made a fortune through his office. He specialized in real estate. Shortly after World War II, Alemán bought a large piece of land on the highway leading north from Mexico City. He paid almost nothing for the property. Then, using his influence as president, he sold parcels of land to middle-class families. The property became *Ciudad Satélite* (Satellite City), a middle-class suburb of the capital. Profits from Satellite City and a plush hotel he owned in Acapulco made Miguel Alemán one of Mexico's richest men.

Alemán reached out to the United States as he sought investments and trade with the giant to the north. Establishing close ties with the

United States was tricky business for a Mexican president. Anti-gringoism (gringo being a slang word for an American) is always present in Mexico. The sentiment waxes and wanes with the times, but America remains the country everyone loves to hate. American bigness and greed are viewed as culprits in most Mexican minds. It is generally believed that huge American companies, if given the chance, will exploit Mexican workers.

In 1947 President Harry Truman visited Mexico City, the first time an American president ever journeyed to the Mexican capital. This was during the Cold War, a period of intense competition between communist and non-communist systems. Alemán resisted communism and Truman approved his stand. At one point during the visit Truman was driven to lay a wreath on the statues of the *Niños Héroes* (Boy Heros). One hundred years earlier the Boy Heroes (cadets at the military school) fought an invading American army and resisted till their deaths. Later in 1947 Alemán came to Washington and made a speech to the U.S. Congress. To the cheers of American lawmakers, the Mexican president said the two countries were united by their, "absolute faith in democracy and essential love for liberty."

The end of Alemán's *sextino* reconfirmed his image as a builder. In his last month in office he attended dedication ceremonies for seven highways, five harbor installations, six irrigation projects, two hospitals, two airports, and a university building. When he retired as president in 1952 relations between the United States and Mexico—the "Distant Neighbors"—were better than ever. Moreover the future looked bright. Mexico appeared to be emerging from its chaotic and impoverished past to take its proper place among the modern, industrial nations of the world.

Artist Robert Fawcett captures a moment of companionship in Mexico's internationally famous Acapulco.

"COKE" IS A REGISTERED TRADE-MARK. COPR. 1957 THE COCA-COLA COMPANY

In exotic
Acapulco... *Here, too, you find The Pause That Refreshes, with ice-cold Coca-Cola.*

Because good taste itself is universal, enjoyment of Coca-Cola has become a welcomed social

custom in over 100 countries. Have a Coke...the

best-loved sparkling drink in all the world.

SIGN OF GOOD TASTE

A 1957 Coca-Cola ad featuring a painting
of Acapulco by artist Robert Fawcett

CHAPTER 5

The Miracle of Mexico

Economists call the thirty year period from 1940 to 1970 "The Miracle of Mexico." On paper, Mexico's progress was indeed miraculous as the economy grew at the rate far exceeding other Latin American countries. Many new factories were started by foreign firms, but national integrity was protected by a law that stated at least 51 percent of a company operating in Mexico had to be owned by Mexicans. Another set of laws put heavy taxes on goods made abroad, thus protecting firms that made products at home. Factory owners were further aided by a cheap and plentiful labor supply because year by year impoverished farmers flooded into the cities seeking work.

Did the bright economic figures mean a higher standard of living for the average Mexican? Critics answered that question with a resounding no. During the "Miracle of Mexico" era the rich got richer while workers and peasants suffered even greater misery than they did in the past. The historian Ramón Eduardo Ruiz called the period "The False Miracle." Writing in 1950, Octavio Paz said, "In absolute numbers there are more rich people [in Mexico] today than there were thirty years ago, but also many more poor people . . . Hence the country's economic development has been notable but its social development most certainly has not. Mexico continues to be a country of scandalous inequities."

Often the measures designed to spur the economy worked against the poor. High tariffs protected Mexican businesses from foreign competition, but they allowed companies to charge what they wished for goods. This situation contributed to inflation, which began during World War II. From 1940 to 1950 the cost of living for working class Mexican families tripled while real wages (money adjusted for inflation) remained roughly the same. Soaring prices did not hamper the rich and their ranks grew. The new rich were not landholders as they were in the past. Now wealthy individuals were bankers, investors, industrialists, and engineers. In the ten-year span after World War II the number of Mexicans classified as millionaires doubled.

While the gap between rich and poor increased, Mexican politics functioned as usual: the PRI always won elections, and the nation's president remained the ultimate boss.

In 1952 Adolfo Ruiz Cortines was sworn in as the new president. Cortines was, of course, a PRI candidate who had been named by Miguel Alemán and party insiders in the customary finger-pointing manner. His election seemed to be a matter of business as usual. But Cortines, even in his acceptance speech, broke long-standing rules. Customarily the incoming president heaped praises upon the outgoing one, as all were members of the PRI club. During his speech, however, Cortines turned toward Alemán and said, "I will not permit the principals of the Revolution nor the laws that guide us to be broken . . . I will be inflexible with public servants who stray from honesty and decency."

It was Cortines's way of declaring official corruption will not be tolerated by his office. From a personal standpoint Cortines was true to his word. A day after taking office he made a public disclosure of everything he owned: a house in Mexico City, a small farm in Veracruz, a modest savings account, and a used Lincoln automobile. He also required all 250,000 federal government employees to issue statements listing their holdings. Cortines made it clear that no federal employee will increase his fortune during his time as president. When he retired from office six years later, Cortines again disclosed his personal possessions. His net worth had increased very little. Usually Mexican presidents retire as wealthy men. Alemán, for example, owned the biggest yacht anchored in Acapulco Bay. In contrast, when Cortines retired he returned to Veracruz to run his modest-size farm.

President Cortines's personal honesty could not stop the corruption that had become so widespread in Mexican society. Paying bribes (*mordidas*) to police, judges, and government clerks was a common practice. In some city neighborhoods homeowners had to pay a *mordida* to garbage collectors if they wanted their trash picked up. Often the people taking bribes did not consider them to be illegal; instead they were looked upon as harmless tips paid for a service rendered. Huge bribes, *mordelones* or "big bites," collected by high officials were thought of as unfair. Still, under-the-counter payments to minor officials continued. Mexicans, most of whom were scrupulously honest in their dealings with others, grudgingly accepted the corruption around them.

In the 1950s American businesses invested and found profits in Mexico: Chrysler, Zenith, and General Electric built factories in the country. Neon signs in all cities lit up the night, flashing the glory of products made by American-owned firms operating in Mexico. Sears, Roebuck and Co. opened its first store in Mexico in 1947 and within ten years had seventeen more branches. Sears offered its valued customers credit cards, a revolutionary innovation which allowed people to buy goods with plastic cards instead of cash.

Due to the influence of its northern neighbor, Mexican culture became Americanized. Television shows made in Hollywood during the 1950s were favorites among Mexican families: *Dragnet*, *Leave it to Beaver*, *The Lone Ranger*. Hot dog vendors replaced taco stands on city streets. Men and women followed baseball with the fervor they once had only for soccer. In many Mexican homes tortillas on the dinner table were replaced with spongy white bread. Nutritionists now

Hugh Beaumont (as Ward Cleaver) and Barbara Billingsley (as June Cleaver) in a scene from *Leave It To Beaver*. Mexican culture became Americanized by influences such as this television show.

claim old-fashioned tortillas are far healthier than white bread, but the attitude at the time said that anything the gringos liked had to be good. The Day of the Dead, the traditional Mexican festival held in October, evolved into a version of American Halloween. Kids dressed up in scary-looking costumes their parents bought at the local American-owned F. W. Woolworth store and knocked on doors in their neighborhood.

Bobby Avila

Baseball had been played in Mexico for generations, but the game did not enjoy nationwide popularity until the 1950s. Bobby Avila from Veracruz was the first Mexican ball player to reach superstar status in the United States. In 1954 Avila, as an infielder for the Cleveland Indians, led the American League with a batting average of .341. When he retired from baseball Avila returned home a hero. Due largely to his baseball fame, he was elected mayor of the city of Veracruz.

In 1957 more than 700,000 American tourists visited Mexico and spent $600 million there. To the American vacationers, Mexico was a bargain. An adequate hotel room could be had for two dollars a night and a first-class hotel was ten to fifteen. Lunch was a dollar and an excellent dinner with wine and dessert might cost five or six. Working-class Mexicans could not dream of paying these "bargain" prices. The man or woman washing dishes in a typical tourist restaurant earned five dollars a week or less.

With the blessings of President Cortines the Mexican peso was devalued and set at a new rate of 12.5 pesos to one dollar. This rate held unchanged for the next twenty years making the peso the most stable currency in all of Latin America. The devaluation further enhanced Mexico as a cheap vacationland for Americans. A bottle of Coca Cola at a lunch stand now cost less than a nickel in American cash.

Americans who visited Mexico in the old days still marvel at the low cost of living. In the 1950s it was possible to live south of the border while spending only five dollars daily.

Acapulco remained a tourist mecca as its beaches and gentle climate attracted thousands of visitors. Impoverished Mexicans flocked to the resort city also, but they looked for jobs instead of fun under the sun. Most job-seekers came from rural areas and were woefully unprepared for city life. Upon arriving at Acapulco, the Mexican poor did not discover the Pacific paradise that greeted tourists. Instead they found a city where far too many people were applying for a limited number of jobs. Many newcomers returned home broken in spirit. Those who stayed joined the city's growing slum communities. Workers lived in tiny shacks made from packing crates, corrugated tin, and even cardboard. Such shantytown settlements developed in the shadows of high-rise hotels, but were almost unnoticed by vacationers. Canadian historian Andrew Sackett studied the city and wrote an essay called *The Two Faces of Acapulco*: "How could tourists come to Acapulco and only see its pleasant side? The architecture of new hotels . . . improved people's experiences by having all the terraces and balconies face the bay—which allowed the aesthetic pleasure of an ocean view but also obscured the teeming, unstable polluted city that was growing only a few hundred meters from the shore."

The movement of people from the country to the cities was one of the major developments of modern Mexico. In 1910, before the Revolution, only 15 percent of the Mexican people lived in cities and towns. By 1960 about half of the population were urban dwellers. The need for jobs triggered this great migration. Only the big farms remained profitable in the 1950s and 1960s. Owners of the large farms could afford to buy tractors and other equipment that lessened their need to employ farm workers. The workers had no choice but to leave the countryside, move to the cities, and hope for the best.

No city grew with the same reckless pace as that of the capital. The population of Mexico City shot up from 1.6 million in 1940 to 3.1 million in 1950 to 5.4 million in 1960. The capital was flooded with newcomers, most of whom were unemployed farmers fresh from the countryside. In their new urban environment they competed for jobs with thousands and thousands of others like them. Mexico City bred slums teeming with the desperate poor.

A notorious slum was Tepito, a district that lay about a ten minute walk from the downtown Zocalo. It was known as a *Bario Bravo* (an angry neighborhood), a high-crime place that was avoided by respectable people. Interestingly, archaeological findings suggest that Tepito was a poor person's section even in Aztec times. In the heart of Tepito stood the *Casa Grande*, an old apartment house whose flats had been divided and subdivided numerous times. In the 1950s Oscar Lewis, an American anthropologist who made intensive studies of slum dwellers, came to *Casa Grande* and interviewed the Sanchez family, a father and four grown children living there. The result was his classic book *Los Hijos de Sanchez* (*The Children of Sanchez*), a sociological study which became a top seller in the United States.

Lewis describes the Tepito neighborhood as, "a poor area with a few small factories and warehouses, public baths, run-down third class movie theaters, overcrowded schools, saloons . . . and many small shops . . . This area ranks high in the incidence of homicide, drunkenness, and delinquency. It is a densely populated neighborhood, during the day and well after dark, the streets and doorways are filled with people coming and going."

Consuelo Sanchez, a daughter who Lewis said "looked thin and pale" told him of an incident she once had in her apartment:

> I remember one morning at the *Casa Grande* an ugly old rat came out of his hole. I was asleep but pretty soon I woke up enough to hear something gnawing under the bed. I opened my eyes wide and hardly breathed, expecting the animal to climb up on the bed. As the sound got closer and closer I began to call my father, at

A poor, elderly grandmother and young children inside
cramped quarters in the overcrowded neighborhood of Tepito

first softly, then a little louder. When I actually heard the animal at the head of my bed I gave a wild scream. My father got up like a flash . . . I kept screaming, 'The rat! The rat!' My brothers got up from their bed on the floor and chased the rat with sticks.

In 1958 Adolfo López Mateos was elected president of Mexico. In his youth he was a pro-labor idealist who supported José Vasconcelos in his 1929 bid for the presidency. As he grew older Mateos became a loyal PRI man. He was perhaps the finest orator of all modern Mexican presidents. Most presidents allowed their young assistants, the *jilgueros* (songbirds), to do their speaking for them. López Mateos not only delivered his own addresses, he also wrote most of them himself, and he was a master at turning flowery Spanish phrases. His commanding presence on speakers platforms combined with his movie star good looks inspired the public. But Mateos suffered numerous health problems which sapped him of his vigor. Once, while giving a speech during the campaign, he was hit with a crushing migraine headache and had to be carried away on a stretcher. Upon taking office the pressures of the presidency diminished his already fragile health.

The 1950s and 1960s were the pinnacle of the "Miracle of Mexico" period. Foreign money flowed in through tourism and international oil sales. In 1963 the International Olympic Committee awarded the Summer Olympics scheduled for 1968 to Mexico City. It marked the first time the Olympic Games were ever to be held in Latin America. International observers were confident that Mexico, despite its troubled past, would handle the Olympic spotlight well.

To the foreign tourists and the business people pouring into Mexico each year, the country seemed at peace with itself. But unknown to the visitors it was a tense peace with unrest simmering just below the surface. In varying degrees the country was a police state during the "Miracle of Mexico" era. Murky laws and a weak court system gave police and the army vast powers which they employed under the guise of keeping order. Labor union officials and students who authorities suspected were potential troublemakers were arrested, often without cause or without a warrant. In jail the "agitators" could be beaten, starved, or even murdered.

Mexico City's Black Palace

A notorious and feared lockup was Mexico City's Lecumberri Prison, a fortress-like building known as the "Black Palace." In the 1960s and 1970s many anti-government men and women died there. The basement held torture rooms where guards used brutal methods to make prisoners talk or to break their will. Said one inmate, "They'd wrap me in cloth like a mummy, tie me to a plank and dunk me in a tub of water until I'd almost drown." In 1976 the Black Palace was closed. The building now houses the Mexican National Archives.

In February 1959 some 60,000 railroad workers went on strike. President López Mateos turned to his secretary of the interior, Gustavo Díaz Ordaz, to settle the dispute. The secretary of the interior had vast powers and was considered to be the nation's "top cop." Dealing with railroad workers put Díaz Ordaz in a precarious position because railroad men were heroes in the Revolution. Railroaders transported Pancho Villa's army over the deserts of northern Mexico, and train crews helped Obregón escape a trap set by rival generals. But now Díaz Ordaz claimed the strike put "our destiny and our history as a country at stake." Acting on Díaz Ordaz's orders, the army took over the railroad system. Some 10,000 workers were arrested. The historian Enrique Krauze wrote, "There were no polite words. They took men down with their clubs and their bayonets."

After several weeks the strike was broken and the railroads ran again. The workers who were arrested spent months in military prisons before they were brought to trial. Two railroad union leaders, both of whom were admitted communists, were imprisoned for ten years. The labor unrest upset President Mateos, who was already in poor health.

During the monthlong strike the president lost forty pounds, and friends claimed he appeared to age ten years.

The railroad strike of 1959 was followed by a teachers' strike and a massive student demonstration. All these protests were broken up with force from the government. Of the student's action, one young college man wrote, "There was a big [student] demonstration due to begin at the teachers' college . . . By eight in the morning the building was surrounded by the mounted police and all kinds of secret agents . . . The mounted police [swinging their clubs] charged the demonstration head-on. Some of us tried to sing the National Anthem but there was no time . . . Forty students who were trapped . . . were the first to fall."

The Death of the Revolution

In 1960 the people of Mexico celebrated the fiftieth anniversary of the start of the Mexican Revolution. For intellectuals and liberals the anniversary was a sad occasion because they felt later governments had betrayed the Revolution's spirit and its aims. In this atmosphere the Mexican novelist Carlos Fuentes published his powerful book *The Death of Artemio Cruz*. The story tells of an aging man, Artemio Cruz, who fought bravely in the Revolution and then spent the rest of his life watching the goals of that struggle disappear. The book won worldwide acclaim and sold well in Mexico.

Relations with the United States remained excellent under President López Mateos. During the 1962 Cuban Missile crisis Mateos sided with the United States. The crisis was triggered when the Soviet Union put guided missiles on Cuban soil. The United States almost went to war as it forced the Soviets to remove the weapons. President Mateos backed U.S. actions, but, in order not to upset left-wing Mexicans, he still had kind things to say about Cuba and its communist leader Fidel Castro.

It came as no surprise when López Mateos pointed at Gustavo Díaz Ordaz and named him the PRI candidate for president.

Díaz Ordaz had served the government well as secretary of the interior, and he kept order during the time of labor and student unrest. The PRI choice won the presidency on September 8, 1964.

Mexican President Adolfo López, right, and Lyndon B. Johnson, left, unveil the new boundary marker signaling the peaceful end of the Chamizal dispute on September 25, 1964. The Chamizal dispute was a border conflict between the U.S. and Mexico over a piece of land between El Paso, Texas, and Ciudad Juárez, Chihuahua.

Sad Fate of López Mateos

A year after leaving office Adolfo López Mateos had a crippling stroke. He was in and out of a coma for six years before he died. The stroke left him—the greatest of all Mexican orators—unable to speak.

Gustavo Díaz Ordaz was born near the city of Puebla in 1911. At one time his family had great wealth and power but lost its riches during the Revolution. When the future president was a teenager his family endured the shame of being evicted from its home due to nonpayment of rent. Despite living in poverty Díaz Ordaz managed to attend college. As a student he was blessed with an excellent memory and an ability to concentrate on details. He later became a university instructor, and he drummed the message home to his students that they must always work to improve their study habits.

In government, Díaz Ordaz was honest and efficient. As a public figure he was the opposite of his predecessor. Where López Mateos was handsome and a brilliant speaker, Díaz Ordaz had an undistinguished voice, and was not handsome. He once made a joke about his unattractive facial features: He told an audience that a rival accused him of being "two-faced," and he responded, "Do you think if I had another face that I would go out on the street with this one?"

President Díaz Ordaz was a fiscal conservative who fretted over Mexico's national budget. Fortunately he served during the "Miracle of Mexico" times when foreign revenue kept the country out of debt. From the beginning he did not want Mexico to host the Olympic Games because he believed the event would cost the nation too much money. The government spent more than 100 million in U.S. dollars to prepare the capital for the games. Upon taking office, he inherited the Olympics, and he was determined to put on a good show. The vast majority of Mexicans backed him in this matter. All knew that in the fall of 1968 Mexico would command the attention of the world.

The late 1960s was a time of unrest in many nations. The Vietnam War, which many young people believed to be an example of American imperialism, raged in Asia. The war killed innocent civilians as well as soldiers. Every day bloody images of suffering in Vietnamese villages were portrayed worldwide on television. This helped to make the U.S. unpopular in Mexico. Tensions peaked in 1968 when issues such as workers' rights and freedom of speech for students sparked riots in places as far away as Chicago and Paris. Now television reporters from around the world descended on Mexico City where leaders began a difficult task: holding a trouble-free Olympic Games in 1968, a year symbolic of revolution.

In July, weeks before the start of the Olympics, two groups of teenage boys played a soccer game in a Mexico City park. The boys did not like each other. Rough play ensued. Someone threw a punch. Fights broke out. Police were called and the boys fled into a vocational school to avoid being arrested. The fracas in the park was a case of hooliganism, certainly not revolution. But the Olympic Games loomed. Commands issued by President Díaz Ordaz and lesser officials told the police to keep order at all costs. Police rushed into the vocational school and began arresting everyone in sight, the rowdy soccer players as well as students who were simply reading in their dorms. Some reports claimed policemen were given cash bonuses for every student they clubbed and dragged outside.

This police reaction—or overreaction—to a street disturbance set off a disastrous chain of events. College students, acting in sympathy with the vocational school, staged a mass march through the streets of Mexico City. Police fired tear gas shells at the marchers. Students threw rocks. For days and nights hit-and-run fights broke out between police and rebellious students.

Baroque Wooden Door

A casualty of the fighting on July 29 was a massive, three-hundred-year-old door on the National Preparatory School, an art school where Rivera and Siqueiros had once attended. The door was world famous for its intricate carvings. Police suspected student rioters were hiding in the school so they blew the ancient door apart with bazooka blasts.

On August 27 some 400,000 demonstrators congregated at the downtown Zocalo. There they pointed to the balcony at the National Palace, the traditional place where the president addresses the public, and called on Díaz Ordaz to make an appearance, saying "Come out on the balcony, loudmouth." Such noisy demonstrations were unusual in Mexico where protest marches were banned and orders issued by police were generally obeyed. Now the demonstrators felt the exhilaration of expressing their feelings while the police despaired over their inability to control the masses.

A large anti-government rally took place on October 2 in Mexico City's Tlatelolco neighborhood, where thousands gathered at a park called Plaza of Three Cultures. Most of those assembled at the park were students, but Tlatelolco was a residential district. Families with children were there also. Everyone noticed the presence of hundreds of young men who, oddly, wore one white glove on their left hands. Spectators did not know who those young men were, but it seemed clear they were not students.

The Plaza of Three Cultures

Mexican school children are taught the history of their country in three periods: ancient times (before the coming of the Spaniards), colonial history (the three hundred years of Spanish rule), and the modern era (beginning with the War of Independence in 1810). Architecture of the three historical stages are seen at the Plaza of Three Cultures where the ruins of an Aztec pyramid stand next to a Spanish-built church and both structures are overshadowed by a modern high-rise building. Nowhere else in Mexico do structures of the three eras come together so neatly as they do in the Plaza of Three Cultures. Also of historical significance, the last battle between Spanish and Aztec soldiers took place in 1521 at what is now Mexico City's Tlatelolco neighborhood.

The Plaza of Three Cultures in Mexico City

Speeches were given and cheers roared from the crowd. Light tanks from the Mexican army ringed the park, but as darkness descended the demonstration was orderly. Then two helicopters began circling above the plaza. They were attack helicopters of the type used in Vietnam, and they bristled with machine guns. People in the crowd watched, nervously, as the helicopters descended to treetop level. Few noticed that most of the men wearing only one white glove had climbed to the third floor balcony of the high-rise building overlooking the park. One of the helicopters dropped two green flares. Then horror broke out on the Plaza of Three Cultures.

Machine gun, pistol, and rifle fire rained down on the crowd. The gunfire came from tanks, the helicopters, and from the gloved men lined up along the balcony. So intense was the gunfire that it sounded like a single explosion. A newspaper reporter in the crowd later wrote, "The hum of bullets caused as much terror as the shooting itself; there were women who hugged their children as they fled . . . The shouts, the weeping, and the desperation were [all] mixed together."

For as long as sixty minutes the firing continued. People tried to flee but the exits to the park were blocked by soldiers brandishing rifles with fixed bayonets. Bodies covered the ground. The wounded screamed. Men and women, frantically trying to escape the murderous fire, knocked each other down and swarmed over those lying on the ground. Said one eyewitness, "The people were trampled; one ran just on top of people."

Finally the shooting diminished. A rain fell, drenching the plaza. Blood ran from the dead in red-stained rivulets. Still the police and the army blocked the exists to the park. It was not until 11:00 in the evening, six hours after the firing started, that ambulances and medics were permitted into the park to treat the wounded. By that time most of the dead bodies had been hauled away in army trucks. Hundreds of men and women, the bystanders as well as the demonstrators, were arrested by police and taken away to jails.

The next day the government said forty-nine people were killed at the plaza. Authorities also claimed student leftists sparked the disorder by firing at police and that the police were forced to return fire. No one explained the significance of the gloved men or the fact that the melee began, as if by signal, with the dropping of two helicopter flares.

Before the eyes of the world the repressive government of Mexico was exposed. Gone was the joyful image of economic progress generated by the Miracle of Mexico. Gone also was the spirit of the Revolution and its promise of democracy and freedom for all. The historian Ramón Edwardo Ruiz wrote, "The massacre of the night of October 2 which occurred in the Plaza de Tlatelolco in Mexico City closed the curtain on the drama of the 'miracle,' laying bare its ugly side."

1968
MEXICO

PUBLISHED AND PRINTED IN HOLLAND © ANTIK PRINT AMSTERDAM P.O.B. 2216

BY COURTESY OF THE MEXICAN OLYMPIC COMMITTEE

A poster of the 1968 Olympic Games in Mexico

CHAPTER 6

Democracy
and
Crisis

The tragedy of Tlatelolco took place just ten days before the Olympic Games were set to begin. In the wake of the massacre some world leaders believed the games should be canceled because further rioting could lead to all-out revolutionary warfare and threaten the safety of the athletes and the thousands who would pour into Mexico City to attend the games. A few international commentators suggested it had been a mistake to hold the Olympics in Latin America, where governments were often unstable and public uprisings frequent. In London the BBC reported, "At this stage it is not clear whether the 7000 athletes, currently preparing for the Games 11 miles away from Tlatelolco in the Olympic Village, are in danger. It is the first time the Olympics have been held in a Latin American country."

Despite concerns, the games began as scheduled, and were a success. Visitors absorbed Mexico's hospitality, its culture, and its food. Though many Mexicans silently cursed their government, they greeted people from abroad in a gracious manner as if they were guests in their own homes.

Torch Bearer

Every Olympics starts with a moment of high drama when an athlete holding a torch races into the stadium and lights the Olympic Flame. In 1968 the honor to carry that torch went to Mexican hurdler Norma Enriqueta Basilio de Sotelo. It marked the first time in the history of the games a woman athlete was chosen to bear the Olympic Torch.

Norma Enriqueta Basilio de Sotelo lighting the Olympic torch in Mexico City on October 12, 1968

Despite the gloom hanging over the country after the tragedy of Tlatelolco, the games gave Mexicans a glorious moment of patriotic pride. A Mexican athlete had never before won a medal in the prestigious track and field events. Then, in the twenty-kilometer race walking contest, three athletes entered the Olympic Stadium to complete their final lap. A Russian led, another Russian was in second, and a Mexican held close behind to cling to third place. This was a shocking development as race walking was not a sport practiced in Mexico. The stadium crowd broke into a chant: "Me-xi-co! Me-xi-co! Me-xi-co!" Slowly, with almost painful tension, the Mexican walker overtook the Russian to win second place and the Silver Medal. Long after the athlete crossed the finish line the crowd continued its roar: "Me-xi-co! Me-xi-co! Me-xi-co!"

Mexican Race Walkers

Race walking is popular in Europe, but the sport never caught on in Mexico before 1968. It is often called heel-and-toe walking because the athlete's leading heel must touch the ground before the trailing toe rises; contact with the ground must be maintained at all times. The Silver Medal winner in 1968, who became a Mexican hero, was José Pedraza, a thirty-one-year-old army sergeant. He trained with the hope of competing, not dreaming he would finish the race in second place. Pedraza's feat inspired other athletes, and Mexico became a race walking powerhouse. A Mexican walker won the Gold Medal in the 1972 Montreal Games, and in 1984 Mexicans captured the Gold and Silver Medal in the twenty-kilometer walk and the Gold Medal in the rugged fifty-kilometer event.

Though the Games were marvelous, no Mexican would forget the tragedy at Tlatelolco and the questions left unanswered: Was the massacre ordered by the president or some other authority? Who were the mysterious men wearing one white glove? Were the flares dropped from the helicopter a prearranged signal for soldiers and police to open fire on the crowd? How many people were actually killed that terrible evening? The government did not provide adequate answers to these perplexing questions. Officials simply told reporters that these matters were "under investigation."

The details, especially regarding the number of men and women killed on the night of October 2, 1968, remain a mystery to this day. Elena Poniatowska, a Mexican journalist, made a painstaking study of the tragedy. She interviewed hundreds of witnesses and published her findings in a book called *La Noche de Tlatelolco* (*The Night of Tlatelolco*). Poniatowska claimed that three hundred to five hundred people were killed. It was also alleged that police picked up many bodies, placed

A photograph taken on October 3, 1968, shows victims of the
Tlatelolco Square Massacre on the floor of Mexico City's main morgue.

them in army trucks, and secretly disposed of them in order to destroy
evidence of a government-ordered massacre.

The pre-Olympic rioting shocked and angered Mexicans. It also
had a long-term effect. A change came over the country that was so
subtle and quiet it was noticed only by Mexicans. In this respect the
transformation was similar to what happened after the Revolution.
Some historians have called Tlatelolco "Mexico's Second Revolution."
In her book, Elena Poniatowska said, "From that moment on, the lives
of many Mexicans were divided in two: before and after Tlatelolco."

As a direct result of Tlatelolco, Mexican society began to open up.
No longer would the people tolerate a dictatorial government or the
rule of a police state. This process took years to fully develop, but the
awful memory of troops gunning down unarmed civilians stayed in
the Mexican conscious. The public now demanded rights enjoyed by
the citizens of other countries: freedom of the press and the freedom to
peacefully assemble topped their demands.

Establishing freedom of the press was the first step in the march to democracy. Mexican apologists claimed that freedom of the press was already in force because the Constitution of 1917 forbade Congress from passing any legislation limiting this essential freedom. It was true that no written law curtailed what Mexican newspapers were permitted to write. But a newspaper that harshly criticized the government or the PRI might get a visit from a government tax collector wanting to see their records. Also a reporter who dared to expose the shady doings of a powerful politician could be accused of slander under the nation's complicated laws, and be involved in a lengthy lawsuit. Fearing such reprisals, the Mexican press tended to be a tame institution. Then came Tlatelolco. Bloodshed at the Plaza of Three Cultures compelled newspapers and reporters to speak out at last.

One crusading journalist was Julio Scherer, a star reporter for the Mexico City newspaper *Excélsior*. Scherer wrote editorials demanding a public investigation of the Tlatelolco tragedy. Other articles in *Excélsior* exposed under-the-table money transactions between politicians and business organizations. This sort of newspaper coverage simply was not done in Mexico. The government countered by canceling its own advertising in *Excélsior*, and many other large companies also reduced their advertising in the paper. *Excélsior*'s circulation dropped as did its profits, but Scherer continued his campaign. The battle between Scherer and the government represented a refreshing break with the past and was appreciated by Mexican intellectuals. Finally a journalist had dared to fight the establishment and demand the right to express a contrary opinion.

One practice that had not changed was Mexico's method of choosing presidents. Díaz Ordaz pointed to fellow PRI man Luis Echeverría, and he became president. Echeverría had been the minister of the interior, the nation's chief law-enforcement officer, and many accused him of orchestrating the massacre at Tlatelolco. The new president hotly denied having anything to do with the killings, but he continued the previous government's policy of discouraging any sort of investigation as to what really went on that evening.

Luis Echeverría saw himself as a populist, a man of the people. He became president on December 1, 1970, and one of his first moves as the nation's chief was to free many of those still held in jail due to the 1968 pre-Olympic uprising. On the international stage he sided with Third World countries and often worked against the interests of the United States.

The historian Enrique Krause called Echeverría "the Preacher" because he often spoke, as if from a pulpit, of his goal to bring greater political freedom to Mexico. In office, however, his actions at times defied his words.

On June 10, 1971, students held demonstrations in Mexico City. The students hoped to revive the nation's student movement which was derailed at Tlatelolco. Some 10,000 protesters marched down a major boulevard when suddenly dozens of young men raced out of buses and attacked the marchers with clubs and chains. Police stood by and watched, doing nothing. The men assaulting the students did not wear uniforms, but it appeared they were following orders and acting on a plan as if they were soldiers. About eleven students were killed and scores wounded.

This disorder did not take place under the limelight of the Olympics so it failed to draw international attention. However the circumstances of the attack on students were eerily similar to what happened at Tlatelolco. Once again government officials failed to explain who the men in the buses were, why they waited along the march route as if poised to commit assault, and why the police did nothing to stop them. The bloody event, which took place on Corpus Christi Day on the Catholic calendar, came to be called the Corpus Christi Massacre.

President Echeverría worked to improve his image as a populist and left-leaning politician. He seized privately owned land in the northern states of Sinaloa and Sonora and, with much fanfare, redistributed the land to peasant farmers. He poured money into massive projects, such as the building of damns and highways. The president determined the lovely Gulf of Mexico port of Cancún should be the next great tourist center, and he directed government funds to construct new roads and

Alfredo Ruiz del Rio, left, and Luis Echeverría Álvarez, right

bridges to serve the city. All these public works cost money. Rather than increase taxes, he raised funds by borrowing from abroad. Mexico's foreign debt rose from $6 billion in 1970, when he took over the presidency, to $20 billion in 1976, when he was ready to leave office.

Economists told Echeverría that Mexico's national debt was so great it would cause the government to have to cancel future public works projects. The president acted by devaluing the peso, a move that stunned the business community. For more than twenty years the Mexican peso exchanged at the rate of 12.5 pesos to one American dollar. This long-standing exchange rate stood as a symbol of Mexico's economic security. Now a devalued peso allowed the country to pay its debts using cheaper money. But the sudden devaluation was an admission by the government that the nation's economy was far more fragile than what was previously believed. To soften the shock, Echeverría's office did not use the word "devaluation." Instead leaders claimed the peso was being allowed to "float" to seek its own value. After several weeks of "floating" the peso stabilized at about 22.5 pesos to the dollar. At first this change was felt mainly by middle-class Mexicans who took frequent trips to the United States and received fewer dollars for their own money. Soon, however, the peso would weaken even more and impact all Mexicans from the wealthy down to the peasants.

In 1976 President Echeverría named José López Portillo to be his successor. The two had long been friends and in their youth had journeyed together to Argentina. Many Mexicans looked at the nomination as an act of cronyism: a pal appointing another pal to high office. It also proved that the system remained unchanged. One man pointed at another man and, quick as one can say *el dedazo* (the big finger, or the fingering of the candidate), that man became president of Mexico.

José López Portillo was a lawyer and a law professor. He was born in Mexico City in 1920 to a moderately wealthy family with a long heritage in Mexico. López Portillo could trace his family roots back to the original five hundred or so Spanish soldiers who conquered Mexico in the 1520s. Being of Spanish heritage allowed him to mingle with Mexico's upper crust. "I was raised in the nobility," he said in his memoirs.

At first López Portillo enjoyed the support of most Mexicans, including the poor. When he became president the country was still jittery over the peso crisis. In traveling about Mexico he displayed an air of calmness and his speeches reflected a confidence in the future. In an interview with the journalist Julio Scherer he claimed to be in control of the economy, and he stated he needed, "three years to pull the country out of its tailspin." He asked Mexicans to bear with him until the economy improved. The majority of Mexicans appeared willing to give their president the time he requested.

Then more oil was discovered along the coast of the Gulf of Mexico. This area had long been an oil-producing region, but now engineers claimed it held vast reserves, similar even to oil-rich Saudi Arabia. The 1970s were a decade when oil was a scarce and expensive commodity. Journalists called petroleum "black gold."

José López Portillo, left, and U.S. President Jimmy Carter,
right, in Mexico City in 1979

Backed by this black gold President López Portillo forgot his patient approach to economic recovery and began a spending spree. A 750-mile-long natural gas pipeline was built running north to the United States, although Mexico had no contracts with the Americans to sell natural gas. The Mexican national oil company, Pemex, built a huge skyscraper in Mexico City financed mainly by the promise of future oil sales. To pay for the building projects the Mexican government fell deeper into debt. Enrique Krause called López Portillo "the gambler" because he encouraged this debt, betting that future oil revenues would allow the nation to pay all its bills. Foreign banks freely gave funds to Mexico for it appeared a state with such vast oil deposits would never default on its loans.

As oil money and foreign loans flowed into the nation, official corruption increased. Corruption reached the highest levels of government. President López Portillo appointed Arturo Durazo, who one historian called "a cheap thug," as his chief of security for Mexico City. Durazo, an old friend of the president, made a fortune by controlling several vices, including drug smuggling to the United States. Powerful members of his police force were themselves a robber gang and became involved in kickbacks, extortion, and kidnappings. Durazo was finally forced to flee the country to avoid arrest. He left behind a mansion outside of Mexico City that included a golf course, several swimming pools, and a private lake. The mansion was valued at $2.5 million. Somehow Durazo managed to buy this luxury house on a police chief's salary of sixty-five dollars a week.

Under López Portillo the Mexican national debt reached $60 billion. The peso grew shakier. Many wealthy Mexicans became *sacadólares*, people who converted their pesos into American dollars they kept in foreign banks. About $14 billion left the country during the six-year reign of López Portillo. The president claimed this practice of sending money out of the country was unpatriotic, because it tightened

Rosa Luz Alegria

In August 1980 President López Portillo named Rosa Luz Alegría secretary of tourism. She was the first woman to attain such a high cabinet post in Mexico. On the surface she seemed to be a brilliant choice as Rosa Luz Alegría was a highly educated physicist. But she proved to be another sad example of López Portillo's cronyism and corruption. Rosa Luz Alegría was the president's mistress. In addition to her prestigious cabinet post, López Portillo gave Rosa Luz Alegría a mansion in Acapulco that was valued at $2 million. Newspapers printed story after story about the president and his well-paid cabinet minister and girlfriend.

the money supply at home and contributed to unemployment. López Portillo further said that Mexican money was basically sound and that he, as the nation's chief, would defend the peso "*como un perro*" (like a dog).

The year 1981 was pivotal for López Portillo and for Mexico. A recession gripped the world, causing widespread unemployment. The price of oil, the black gold Mexico counted on for its future, dropped dramatically. The head of Pemex reduced Mexican oil by four dollars a barrel in order to make it competitive in the overseas marketplace. The move angered the president and López Portillo fired the Pemex chief and changed the reduction to two dollars a barrel. The meager price cut did little to spur sales. Mexico found itself paying heavy interest on foreign loans and unable to find customers for its petroleum.

In September 1982 President López Portillo made a shocking series of announcements. One, Mexico could no longer make payments on its international loans. Two, the banks were to be nationalized and rules were to be established making it impossible for depositors to change their money into dollars. Three, the peso was to be devalued once again.

López Portillo claimed these moves were forced upon him and that he was not to blame for the current crisis. The situation, he said, was largely the fault of the *sacadólares* who greedily stashed their money in foreign, mostly American, banks. In one speech he likened himself to a sea captain and cried out, "I was responsible for the helm but not for the storm." His PRI associates praised the president for his heroism in making such tough decisions. Some political supporters compared López Portillo's nationalization of the banks to the boldness of Lázaro Cárdenas nationalization of the oil industry in 1938.

But few average Mexicans accepted López Portillo's defense. His downgrading of the peso was particularly galling because it came shortly after the president bragged he would defend the Mexican currency "like a dog." According to an unconfirmed but often told story, López Portillo took his wife to an elegant Mexico City restaurant the night he

A Mexican peso

announced the devaluation. Wealthy Mexicans tend to be dignified and possess Old World manners, but the collapse of the peso unnerved everyone. According to the story, as the presidential couple studied the restaurant menu, several fellow diners turned to their table and made barking noises: "Arf! Arf! Woof! Woof!"

Buildings shrouded in smog in Mexico City

CHAPTER 7

What went Wrong?

Miguel de la Madrid became president in 1982. The new president was a banker who had studied at Harvard University in the United States. He took over a country on the brink of economic meltdown. The devalued peso made foreign goods and many domestically produced products more expensive than ever before. Inflation approached 100 percent a year. Spiraling prices caused greater suffering for poor people and sharply reduced the standard of living once enjoyed by the middle class.

López Portillo's Retirement

Mexicans heaped the blame for their economic miseries on past president José López Portillo. The situation at home became so uncomfortable for López Portillo that he escaped to Europe to spend his retirement years. He could afford the vacation. When López Portillo began as president he was considered to be a man of moderate wealth. When he left office six years later his total worth was estimated at between $1 billion and $3 billion, making him one of the country's richest men.

Miguel de la Madrid called for austere measures to fix the economy. To bring inflation under control, the president canceled many expensive public works projects. This, of course, meant fewer jobs. Poor people grumbled that it was the rich and powerful who brought the country into this deplorable situation and now the poor were asked to tighten their belts in order to fix it. Still, most Mexicans backed their new president and hoped for better times.

Mexican rural areas had long been the most impoverished sections of the country. Now, with the peso crisis and the austerity program, the rural areas became worse. Farm workers and small farmers, unable to make a living off the land, were forced to move to the urban areas whether they wanted to or not. Fields in the country grew tangled with weeds while Mexico's cities and towns swelled.

Mexico City received the bulk of migrants. In the 1980s people moved to the capital in such great numbers and so rapidly they were called *paracaidistas* (parachutists) because it seemed they just dropped from the sky. Acting as a magnet to the newcomers was a suburb with the tongue-twisting Aztec name Nezahualcoyótl. Six hundred years earlier the Aztec poet and emperor Nezahualcoyótl lived on these grounds. In modern times Neza (as its residents called it) became a stunning example of the Mexico City region's population explosion.

Mexican Urbanization

The rush to the cities continued after World War II when rural dwellers could no longer make a living doing farm work. All Mexican cities and towns experienced rapid growth. Below is a decade-by-decade breakdown of Mexico's urbanization since 1950:

1950....42.70 % of the people were urban dwellers
1960....50.80 % urban
1970....59.00 % urban
1980....66.30 % urban
1990....72.50 % urban
2000....74.70 % urban

Source: U.N. Common Database (U.N. Population Division Estimates)

Neza was a barren, rocky land devoid of houses as late as 1950. Then the rural economy collapsed, and hoards of farm folk flocked to the cities, especially to the capital area. In just a few years Neza was home to 1.5 million people and was the nation's fifth-largest municipality. At first the suburb was a deplorable slum, a confusing sprawl of lean-to shacks built from scrap tin and crates. But impoverished Mexicans have ingenious ways of improving their communities by taking small steps. Families planted flower gardens and put up window boxes sprouting plants. Gradually tin walls came down to be replaced by cinder blocks. Neza, which lies near Mexico City's busy Benito Júarez Airport, became a livable and even a loved district.

Between 1960 and 1980, Mexico City's population more than doubled. Because of the constant influx from the country, the capital expanded to the point where Mexico City and its immediate surroundings held approximately 25 percent of the entire Mexican population. Various studies ranked Mexico City as one of the three most populous urban areas in the world.

Greater Mexico City's environment paid a heavy price for its runaway growth. The capital was an industrial hub as well as the center of government. By the 1980s Mexico City was home to 30,000 factories and almost 3 million motor vehicles. Cars and industries poured more than 11,000 tons of gaseous wastes into the air each day. Mexico City lies in a valley ringed by mountains so the foul gases had no place to escape. The capital gained the dubious distinction of having the worst air pollution of any city in the world. Windless days found the city covered with smog so thick it was impossible to see across the street. Cars had to drive with their lights on even in broad daylight. Residents, especially children, suffered from eye ailments and from asthma.

The Miracle of the Metro

Vehicle traffic was diminished somewhat by the development of Mexico City's excellent subway system. The metro opened in 1969 with one line and sixteen stations. Workers had to be especially careful digging the underground portions because beneath modern Mexico City lies the ruins of the wondrous Aztec capital, Tenochtitlán. A team of archaeologists accompanied each work crew as they dug. Near the Zocalo the diggers discovered an altar dedicated to the god Ehécatl. The altar was preserved and riders at the Pino Suárez station now gaze across the track and see this ancient structure as they wait for their train. Mammoth bones were found while digging the Talismán Station, and they too were preserved as an exhibit. By the year 2010 the Metro had expanded to include eleven lines, 163 stations, 280 miles of track, and it served more than 4.5 million riders each day. The Metro is the second-largest subway in North America, trailing only New York City.

The altar dedicated to Ehécatl in the Pino Suarez subway station

The capital was also the site of the greatest natural calamity to strike Mexico in its modern history. It was a pivotal event which saw people dating their lives into periods before and after the disaster.

September 19, 1985, dawned as an ordinary day in the capital. By sunrise the streets were locked in their usual morning traffic jams. However a gentle breeze blew away the worst of the air pollution that day and a cheerful-looking sun rose. Then, just after 7 a.m., tall buildings swayed like trees bending in the wind. Windows broke and jagged glass rained down on the sidewalks. Upon feeling the sidewalk wobble at their feet people walking about outside shouted, "*Terremoto! Terremoto!*" "Earthquake! Earthquake!"

Mexico City lies on shaky ground. Most city dwellers had experienced minor earthquakes in the past, but this was no minor quake. The earthquake of 1985 was one of the strongest ever recorded. The tremor measured 8.1 on the Richter scale (10 is the highest number), and it was felt as far away as Houston, Texas, 1,100 miles to the north. High-rise buildings along Mexico City's boulevards collapsed inwardly like accordions. Ten-story buildings were in minutes reduced to four-story piles of rubble. A resident living on an upper floor of one apartment building claimed he felt a tickling feeling in his stomach as if he were riding downward on an elevator when his high-rise flattened out. A government worker, his wife and two children were having breakfast in their four-story building when, "All of a sudden the shaking began," said the man. "Trying to calm my daughter, I shouted for my wife to join us. We embraced tightly. Only by pretending to protect them could I control my terror. Things fell all around us and the windows shattered. After what seemed an eternity the trembling stopped. We were alive . . . [My wife] turned her head slowly to the window. 'Oh my God, look,' she said . . . And we saw the massive cement structure [next door] collapsing like a castle of cards."

When the dust settled almost four hundred buildings in the heart of Mexico City were wrecked. People were trapped inside and when the fires started men and women imprisoned in the wreckage screamed for help. Individual policemen and fire fighters dug their way through

The 1985 Mexico City earthquake destroyed this eight-story structure

the debris to rescue the entrapped, but for the most part city officials performed dismally. Many local functionaries were PRI appointees who got their positions through loyalty to the party rather than their own competence. Now they seemed to be overwhelmed with the calamity facing them. Said one city manager, "This goes way beyond me. I have to await instructions."

While city officials were paralyzed with indecision, ordinary men and women sprang into action. Risking their own safety, volunteers sifted through piles of knife-like glass and broken drywall to reach survivors. They put out fires by whatever means they could. In the days to come the volunteers became the city's only government. College students led the way. One student, Imanol Ordorika, said, "The city was ours. We were in control. We directed traffic in the streets. We commandeered public buses when we needed them. We organized the food lines in damaged neighborhoods."

No survivor would ever forget the Day of the Quake. At least 9,000 people were killed (some reports put the number of dead at 20,000), 30,000 were injured, and 95,000 were left homeless. The cost of quake damage was estimated at between 3 and 4 billion U.S. dollars. There was a pattern to the destruction. Churches and other buildings put up three hundred years earlier by the Spaniards suffered only minor damage. The forty-five story Latin American Tower (completed in 1956) also withstood the earthquake. However, many of the structures constructed in the 1960s and 1970s, when the capital doubled in population, collapsed. Lax building laws written to accommodate rapid expansion led to most of the death and destruction of September 1985.

Miguel de la Madrid served his six years as president and retired in 1988. He was not loved by the people, but neither was he hated. At least he did not retire in disgrace as did López Portillo. The policies favored by Madrid slowed, but did not halt, the country's crippling inflation. The peso continued its decline, trading at 925 to the dollar when Madrid left office.

Carlos Salinas de Gortari, was named as the PRI candidate for president in 1988. Salinas was a loyal PRI man, chosen in the usual finger-pointing manner. His election was thought to be certain as the PRI always won. But the political climate in Mexico had changed. Inflation, rampaging poverty, and the government's abysmal response to the earthquake enraged voters. Mexicans were determined to make the election of 1988 a giant step toward change. And this time the people had a viable opposition candidate.

Cuauhtémoc Cárdenas was the son of Lázaro Cárdenas, the beloved ex-president. He had served as senator from the state of Michoacán and was a trained engineer. He did not show emotions readily and was uninspiring as a public speaker but he had a magical last name.

Cuauhtémoc Cárdenas was once a PRI member, but he grew weary of that party's inside dealings and its undemocratic practices. In 1988 he became head of an organization called the Democratic National Front, a coalition of small left-of-center parties.

What's in a Name: Cuauhtémoc

Cuauhtémoc is a rather common first name given to boys in Mexico. The name is rich in history: Cuauhtémoc, the last Aztec emperor, had led his nation in battle against the Spaniards in the 1520s. Another famous namesake is Cuauhtémoc Blanco, a star player in Mexican soccer.

Early returns on election day July 6, 1988, saw Cárdenas climb ahead with a substantial lead. This development stunned PRI leaders who believed it was impossible for an opposition candidate to beat their chosen man. But the returns kept coming in, and they indicated Cárdenas was about to score a remarkable victory. Then, late in the evening as the public expected to hear official word that Cárdenas was the new president, a government spokesman appeared on television and made a terse statement: *se cayó el sistema* (the system, meaning the vote-counting computer, failed). Because of this "failed system" the announcement of the election results had to be delayed.

Several days later the system was miraculously restored. The votes were tallied and Carlos Salinas de Gortari of the PRI was declared to be the winner. Because the entire vote-counting organization was, as everyone knew, controlled by PRI insiders, most Mexicans suspected fraud—that the election of 1988 had been stolen by the party in power. Salinas took office and, as if to confirm the charge of fraud, ordered all the paper ballots completed on voting day to be burnt. The statement about "the system" became a cynical joke told especially in college classrooms. If a student failed a test badly and the instructor asked why the student simply said: *se cayó el sistema*.

Octavio Paz - Nobel Laureate

All of Mexico felt proud in 1990 when Octavio Paz won the Nobel Prize for Literature. Paz was born in Mexico City in 1914. During the Revolution his father served as an advisor to Emiliano Zapata. Paz, educated in Europe and in the United States, was both an essayist and a poet. He once called poetry, "the secret religion of the modern age." His most celebrated book, *The Labyrinth of Solitude* (first published in 1950), is an examination of Mexican society. In many of his writings Paz was sharply critical of the Mexican leaders, their corruption, and their dictatorial practices. Paz once served his government as ambassador to India, but he resigned in protest in 1968 because of the Tlateloco Massacre.

The Salinas presidency started badly with the controversial election, and matters soon became worse. On January 1, 1994, an armed rebellion broke out in the southern state of Chiapas, an impoverished region populated mostly by Maya Indians. A rebel army, whose soldiers called themselves Zapatistas after the revolutionary leader Emiliano Zapata, took over several Chiapas cities. The Zapatistas were led by an enigmatic man who wore a mask and called himself Subcomandate Marcos. The Chiapas rebels demanded a separate state and greater independence for Mexico's indigenous people.

Mexicans at the time of the Zapatista uprising were in a bitter mood. Many believed they lived under an unelected president. Subcommandante Marcos, always wearing a mask, appeared on television news programs where he uttered revolutionary statements. He became a hero to many when he said the government was made up of bandits and cowards. In contrast, Marcos seemed to be a man of convictions. In the popular imagination he became the Robin Hood of modern Mexico. President Salinas sent army units into the Chiapas. Fire fights broke out between the Zapatistas and the soldiers. Scores were killed on both sides. The battles were indecisive, because the Zapatistas were skilled at melting into the Chiapas forests to avoid capture.

In 1994 Mexico, the U.S., and Canada entered into the North American Free Trade Agreement (NAFTA). Under NAFTA policy, tariffs on goods made in the three countries would be reduced and eventually eliminated. The agreement encouraged the growth of factories along the Mexican side of the border. These factories, called maquiladoras, were mostly owned by American companies. They employed Mexicans who were paid considerably less than what U.S. workers earned. By the mid-1990s more than 2,000 maquiladoras operated near the border, employing about 500,000 Mexicans.

Carlos Salinas never gained the trust of Mexicans. Many called him "*Señor*" Salinas, pointedly refraining from using the words *Señor Presidente*. The situation worsened as Salinas often conferred with his brother, Raúl Salinas, when pondering matters of national importance.

Raúl Salinas was a wealthy businessman often condemned as a ruthless individual who would stop at nothing in his pursuit of money and power. There was talk that Raúl engaged in money laundering for the drug cartels, which were growing in Mexico. This was confirmed, in part, in 1992, when Carlos Enrigue Cervantes de Gortari (a cousin and close associate of Raúl) was convicted of drug trafficking in the United States and sentenced to fifteen years in prison.

Those who wished to break the power of Salinas and his group put their hopes on Luis Donaldo Colosio from the state of Sonora. Although Colosio was a PRI member, he had a greater world view than the average party loyalist. Colosio was weary of the PRI being, in essence, the government of Mexico. In March 1994 he made a shocking speech, in which he called Mexico an impoverished country whose progress was impeded by corrupt politicians. The speech created a sensation. Mexican leaders, especially those connected with the PRI, had never condemned their government in such brutal terms.

Two weeks after the controversial speech, Colosio walked among crowds while shaking hands at a political rally in the city of Tijuana. A man approached him on foot and shot him dead. Police arrested the gunman, Mario Aburto Martínez, a twenty-three-year-old unemployed factory worker. Many Mexicans believed the murder and arrest was a cover-up for higher crimes. It was said there were more than one gunman and that government figures, or possibly Raúl Salinas, ordered the killing. None of these widespread beliefs could be proven. The arrested man, who behaved as if he were confused and mentally out-of-balance, was sentenced to life in prison. He never admitted he was part of a larger conspiracy.

President Salinas's *sextino* ended on December 1, 1994. A new president, Ernesto Zedillo of the PRI, took command. He faced an immediate crisis: foreign investors were reluctant to put money into a country that appeared so unstable. Days after taking office, Zedillo took all controls off the peso and allowed it to seek its own level. Salinas called this decision by the new president *el error de diciembre* (the December mistake). But many critics claimed Salinas's denunciation of the move was his attempt to dodge blame for the country's chaotic economy.

The Salinas Legacy

After his presidential term Carlos Salinas took up residence in Ireland and later in London. Often he disappeared for months at a time, and no one knew his whereabouts. Raúl Salinas, the ex-president's brother, was arrested for his alleged role in the assassination of José Francisco Ruiz Massieu, a PRI leader. Another Salinas brother, Enrique Salinas, was found dead in his car in 2004 near Mexico City. It was rumored that Enrique had made deals with drug cartel members, double-crossed them, and was murdered as a result. The murders and alleged gangster connections associated with the ex-president's family made newspaper headlines for years. Today historians generally regard the Carlos Salinas presidency as the most corrupt in modern Mexico's history.

Toward the end of the Salinas *sextino* the Mexican peso exchanged at the rate of 3,375 to the dollar. Prices for all goods skyrocketed. A bottle of Coca Cola at a grocery store cost one thousand pesos. A shoe shine at a stand cost 2,000 pesos, or 2,000 times more than that same service cost just fifteen years earlier. The peso, once thought of as the most stable currency in all of Latin America, had been devalued to the point where it was next to worthless.

President Ernest Zedillo, who began his term in 1994, took over a demoralized country. An armed rebellion was brewing in the south, a reform candidate for president was murdered on a city street, and no one had faith in the national currency. Those who studied the history of modern Mexico remembered the periods of hope such as the spirit of the Revolution and the promise of the miracle years. Now Mexicans asked: What went wrong? What in the world went wrong?

A Samaritan worker walking down a dirt road near Arivaca, Arizona.
A trail used by illegal immigrants crosses the road up ahead.
Food and water are left along the trail as a humanitarian gesture.

CHAPTER 8

The Lure of El Norte

Wages for workers increased in the 1990s, but the pay hikes never matched the new and baffling cost of living. Poor people now ate little more than tortillas and beans. The middle class, which had been growing stronger since the 1960s, was all but wiped out by the peso crisis. Rich men and women kept the bulk of their money in dollar accounts tucked safely away in U.S. banks, and they survived the tough times with relative ease. They even developed a new toast. At cocktail parties wealthy people clinked their glasses together and said, "To Mexico, still the greatest country in the world to be rich in."

For American tourists with dollars in their pockets the devalued peso made a Mexico vacation a bargain once more. Dollar prices dwindled almost to their level of the 1950s. A hotel cost six or seven dollars a night and a meal at a restaurant two dollars. Impoverished Mexicans saw the tourists from *el norte* spending pesos as if they meant nothing and grew resentful. Their anger was directed not at the tourists, but instead at Mexican leaders whose policies had devastated the country.

Near the border sprawled the maquiladoras. In the mid-1990s a new maquiladora factory building opened almost every day. Writers began calling the border region the Maquiladora Nation. Mexican factory workers earned about one-tenth the pay scale of factory hands in the United States. Most maquiladora workers were women. The plants were devoted to the assembly of devices such as electric razors and radios, and it was reasoned women had the small and delicate hands ideal for such work. Also, as had long been the case, Mexican women earned far less than men. There were no effective laws requiring equal pay for the sexes and plant owners were free to pay women lower wages.

Women workers at the Universal Scientific Industrial de Mexico plant in Guadalajara, Mexico, assemble computer motherboards for export to the United States.

Maquiladoras in the city of Ciudad Juárez, which lies across the Rio Grande from the Texas town of El Paso, employed 180,000 young women in the late 1990s. Many of the women came from the south with their husbands and children. The women found jobs in the assembly plants quickly while the men endured unemployment.

The maquiladora nation began to crumble near the year 2000 due to, ironically, the wages paid to assembly plant workers. As badly as Mexican factory hands were paid, workers in China and Indonesia were paid even less. The border factories began relocating to Asia. In 2001 and 2002 some 529 maquiladors closed their Mexican operations and opened new facilities across the Pacific. Because of the closings more than 228,000 people lost their jobs.

For the Mexican poor there was a last resort: *el norte*, the United States. The journey was difficult and often dangerous but impoverished people reasoned it had to be made. Legally or illegally millions of Mexicans immigrated to the United States during the decade of the 1990s.

As the Mexican economy teetered, workers looked to jobs in *el norte* as their only course of action. *El norte* became the economic salvation for individual Mexicans and it served as a safety valve for the nation. If masses of desperate workers had to stay at home and cope with the weak economy riots and disorder might break out.

The United States proudly calls itself "a nation of immigrants." From its beginnings the country has taken in new citizens from abroad. The Statue of Liberty stands in New York harbor as a symbol of this welcoming spirit. Between 1991 and 2000 11 million immigrants from all nations were accepted under the law and settled into the United States. No other country has such generous immigration policies.

However, becoming a legal resident of the United States was a daunting task for an impoverished Mexican. An applicant for legal papers must wait at least six months for a visa to be issued. Just to apply for a visa costs more than one hundred dollars and the applicant can be turned down for dozens of reasons. Many Mexicans believed they

The Rio Grande forms part of the border between the U.S. and Mexico. The terrain is difficult to navigate.

could not go through this lengthy and expensive practice. So the poor entered the United States *abajo alumbre* (under the barbed wire). This meant crossing the border without being detected by the U.S. Border Patrol.

The first task for the undocumented worker was to enlist the services of a *coyote* also called a *pollero* (chicken herder). A *pollero* serves as a guide and takes groups of migrants through the border to the United States. A skilled guide knows all the weak spots along the border, places where there are holes in the border fence and stretches of land where there are fewer border police. *Coyotes* are often thought of as criminals who have little regard for laws, customs, or the rights of others. But this is not always the case. One *coyote* was interviewed by the American journalist Judith Adler Hellman. She called him Pedro P.

"There's nothing slick about Pedro," Hellman wrote, "he looks like the people he guides to the other side." Pedro grew up in the border city of Tijuana. As a teenager he began sneaking across the border to take dishwashing jobs in southern California restaurants. Eventually Pedro chose the full-time job of guiding illegals to the other side. "In the ten years I've worked as a *pollero*," he said, "I've brought thousands of people across—men, women, and children." He takes pride in his work. "My business is based on trust, on recommendations of people I have passed to the other side. Folks come to me because I have a reputation for skill and reliability." When this interview was conducted, in the late 1990s, Pedro charged his followers between 250 to three hundred dollars to deliver them to the United States. This price has since increased tenfold because border conditions such as fences and patrols get stronger with each passing year.

If caught by the Border Patrol the undocumented person is detained while authorities check to see if he or she is accused of any crimes in the U.S. Those who have no criminal record are put on buses and sent back to Mexico. Many have crossed the border back and forth dozens of times before.

Boxcar Horror

Border Patrol agents searched a railroad yard in Sierra Blanca, Texas, in 1987 when they heard a faint cry: "*Ayuda me. Ayuda me.*" ("Help me. Help me"). The patrolmen opened a locked boxcar and made a horrific discovery: inside were the bodies of eighteen Mexican immigrants and one man who was barely alive. A *coyote* had put the immigrants in the train on the Mexican side promising them an associate would free them once the car was parked in U.S territory. The *coyote* locked the door and the boxcar joined a train which crossed the border. However the associate never arrived to open the door and release the trapped people. Temperatures within the car reached 130 degrees F, and air for breathing was exhausted. The lone survivor managed to punch a breathing hole in the car's floor with a railroad tie. The other migrants suffered what had to be terrible deaths.

During the 1990s the U.S. enjoyed a strong economy and undocumented persons could find jobs with relative ease. They took low-wage jobs cleaning toilets in hospitals or picking crops under the broiling sun. It was a violation of U.S. law to knowingly hire an undocumented worker, but the law was often ignored.

The typical undocumented worker was a young man with a wife and perhaps two children at home in Mexico. If the young man was responsible he regularly sent checks to his family. Those checks, called remittances or *remesas* in Spanish, became an important factor in the Mexican domestic economy. In the 1990s remittances were the second greatest source of income for the nation.

Many Americans resented the influx of undocumented immigrants and felt they were taking jobs away from American citizens. There were also concerns about the dangers of having millions of people in the country without documentation.

The U.S. Congress appropriated money to strengthen its border with Mexico. Between 1994 and 1998 the budget for the Border Patrol doubled. Stronger fences were built all along the 2000-mile border and more officers were hired. The new measures made a crossing more difficult and more dangerous, but the migrants kept coming. They waded across the Rio Grand and climbed barbed wire barriers. They crawled through sewer pipes. They endured freezing nights in the windswept Arizona deserts. They hid in shipping crates, car trunks, and railroad boxcars to make the crossing. A University of Houston study claimed 3,000 undocumented men and women died trying to reach the United States from 1995 to 2000.

In 1986 the U.S. Congress passed an immigration reform law which granted amnesty to anyone who had entered the country illegally and had been in the country for more than four years. The undocumented person had to prove he or she had a record of regular employment and had committed no major crimes. During the 1990s 2.7 million people from all countries were awarded citizenship under the new law.

The 1986 immigration law did not solve the problem, however. The Mexican economy continued to weaken as the new century began. And, more people trekked to *el norte*, although the journey presented ever greater hazards. To most Mexicans it was a matter of simple arithmetic. A man pushing a wheel barrel at a construction site in Mexico earned six or seven dollars a day, whereas the same work north of the border paid that much an hour. It was a matter of survival.

Police at the Mexican Drug Enforcement Agency stand in formation, while smoke fills the air from burning bags of cocaine confiscated from drug dealers.

CHAPTER 9

Change and Peril

Ernesto Zedillo served as Mexico's president from 1994 to 2000. He grew up in the state of Baja California, where his father was an auto mechanic. Despite his humble origins Zedillo earned advanced degrees in economics at Yale University in the United States. The president's background as an economist served him well as he tried to resolve Mexico's peso crisis. Working with American president Bill Clinton, Zedillo arranged a $50 billion international loan. The money was used to pay pressing foreign debts and to help stabilize the peso. Mexico repaid its loan ahead of schedule and the peso gained strength. From the late 1990s to 2010 Mexico's currency traded at between nine and thirteen pesos to the dollar. Inflation—at least the wild, crazy inflation of the past—diminished.

President Zedillo talked about bringing greater democracy to Mexico, but such talk was nothing new. Many presidents said the same thing. Then, toward the end of his term, Zedillo made two significant moves. First he strengthened the Federal Election Institute, making it far more difficult for powerful politicians to rig the vote count. Next he instituted a system of primary elections. This meant the practice of the *dedazo*, the finger-pointing method of naming a new president, was over. The very idea of primary elections shocked veteran members of the PRI, Zedillo's own party. Now they had to ponder the unthinkable: perhaps, in the future, a PRI candidate for president could lose.

Voting day came July 2, 2000, and three men ran for president: Francisco Labastida of the PRI, Cuauhtémoc Cárdenas representing the Party of the Democratic Revolution (PRD), and Vicente Fox of the *Partido de Acción National* (the Party of National Action or PAN). Vicente Fox and the PAN won the presidency with 42 percent of the vote. This time the voting process was clean, honest, and democratic. The three candidates even held televised debates, U.S. style, before the general election. Not all Mexicans agreed that Fox

Vicente Fox

was the best leader for the country, but all understood the election was a historic step forward. For the first time in seventy-one years the PRI lost a presidential contest. The era of one-party rule was over. Mexico was, at last, a true democracy.

Vicente Fox grew up in a well-to-do family in the state of Guanajuato and was educated at the Harvard Business School in the United States. As a young man, Fox worked for the Coca-Cola Company as a sales representative. He worked his way up to become a regional president and helped to make Coca-Cola Mexico's top-selling soft drink. In 1995 he was elected governor of Guanajuato. As governor he instituted a policy of making public all state financial transactions in order to discourage corruption.

At six-foot-five, Fox was perhaps the tallest president in Mexican history. He once lived on a large family-owned ranch and remained a rancher at heart, dressing in cowboy garb complete with boots and a wide-brimmed hat. Fox was a gifted speaker and was well-liked even by those who disagreed with his policies. Establishing greater democracy was the theme of his *sextino*. This meant he tolerated splinter groups. Fox even reached out to the Zapatistas and allowed their masked leader, Subcomandate Marcos, to address the congress.

However, the plight of the Mexican worker did not improve under Vicente Fox. In 2004 the minimum wage mandated by law was forty-five pesos a day in Mexico City. This daily wage (and many employers broke the law and paid their help even less) bought a Big Mac and fries in one of the city's McDonald's restaurants. Thus a worker's entire daily salary could be spent buying lunch.

Impoverished Mexicans continued to look to *el norte* as their only salvation. Between 2000 and 2004 at least 500,000 Mexican crossed the border illegally each year. The September 11, 2001, terrorist attacks on the United States caused the American government to tighten security at the border. Although no Mexican participated in the attacks, it was reasoned that if undocumented workers could slip over the southern border so could international terrorists. Border security became a pressing issue in the United States. Even short term visas, which allowed a Mexican to vacation in the United States or visit a relative there, became difficult to obtain. Still the immigrants—the legal ones as well as the illegals—came.

Controversial Law

In April 2010 the state of Arizona passed the nation's sternest law aimed at deporting immigrants who entered the state illegally. The law allows police to stop and demand identification papers from people who look Hispanic. It did not matter if the Hispanic-looking person was from a family that had lived in the U.S. for one hundred years. Anyone could be detained by the police due to facial features and skin color alone. Many Americans denounced Arizona's anti-immigrant law. The Catholic Cardinal Roger M. Mahony of Los Angeles claimed the measure was akin to "Nazism."

In 2006 Felipe Calderón was elected president of Mexico. He was a PAN member and served under Fox as Mexico's secretary of energy. His major opponent was López Obrador of the PRD. The election was the closest on record with Calderón winning by less than a 1 percent margin. López Obrador demanded the votes be recounted, saying he was the real winner. For a few tense months two men claimed the presidency, and in the past this situation could devolve into internal warfare. But Mexico had acquired greater political maturity and the matter was resolved peacefully. Inspectors determined that despite a few irregularities the vote count was honest and accurate. Felipe Calderón took office without incident.

Felipe Calderón at the World Economic Forum Annual Meeting in Grabünden, Switzerland, on January 30, 2009

Presidents of Mexico Since 1952

Adolfo Ruiz Cortines (years in office 1952-1958)

Adolfo López Mateos (1958-1964)

Gustavo Díaz Ordaz (1964-1970)

Luis Echeverría (1970-1976)

José López Portillo (1976-1982)

Miguel de la Madrid (1982-1988)

Carlos Salinas de Gortari (1988-1994)

Ernest Zedillo (1994-2000)

Vicente Fox (2000-2006)

Felipe Calderón (2006-)

The new president faced a major problem: the drug wars that were heating up, especially in the northern part of the country. Mexican narcotics gangs smuggled illegal drugs—cocaine, heroin, and marijuana—over the border to their contacts in the United States. Americans consume more illegal drugs than the citizens of any other nation in the world. The business of drug smuggling was fantastically lucrative, bringing Mexican narco gangs an estimated $14 billion a year. Gang leaders had fabulous life-styles complete with luxury houses, cars, and clothing. However the drug kingpins were never able to truly enjoy these riches. Gangs fought rival gangs for territory and for influence over local police departments. The gang leaders' houses stood like fortresses and were surrounded by private armies.

Combat in the drug wars took place near the border, where narcotics were smuggled to the other side. It was a vile conflict that saw opposing gangs torturing and executing captives in order to instill fear among their opponents. Headless bodies were found along rural highways in the north, left there to serve as messages as to which gang is in charge of this territory. Early in his administration President Calderón issued what amounted to a declaration of war against the narco gangs. The president was aware that local police forces were not effective in stopping drug activity because the gangs had infiltrated law enforcement agencies. Calderón ordered the army into northern Mexico. Calderón's use of the army intensified the fighting. In the first four years of his administration an estimated 28,000 people were killed in drug-related violence.

New Mayor

In October 2010 the town of Práxedis G. Guerrero in the northern state of Chihuahua got a new police chief in Marisol Valles García, a twenty-year-old female. This was unprecedented since Mexican police chiefs were almost universally middle-age men. But so many department heads have been killed by drug lords in northern Mexico that no man wanted the job. In Práxedis G. Guerrero, a township of 8,500 people, gang members consider it fun to ride up and down the streets firing pistols out of their car windows. "This is a town without law," said one resident, "Let's see what a woman can do . . . things can't get any worse."

The drug wars raging in northern Mexico made the journey of undocumented workers even more dangerous. Drug gangs routinely stopped the migrants and charged them fees to travel on their "turf." Often the narco merchants forced undocumented people to work as "mules," carrying drugs across the border and delivering them to gang members on the other side. All the migrants knew that if the Border Patrol caught them transporting drugs they could be sentenced to many years in a U.S. prison, but it was not an option to simply say no. Those who refused to work as mules were beaten or shot.

On August 23, 2010, a drug gang stopped a group of seventy-two migrants and shot them all to death. This massacre took place near the town of San Fernando, just one hundred miles from the U.S. border. The reason behind the executions was unclear. Perhaps the migrants resisted working as mules, perhaps they declined to pay the fee demanded by the narco gang, or perhaps gang members simply wanted to commit mass murder to terrorize the next group of travelers unlucky enough to cross their territory.

Recent years have seen a decline in the number of immigrants coming into the U.S. illegally. In 2009 the PEW Hispanic Center said 11.1 million undocumented people lived in the United States, down from a peak of 12 million in 2007. Fear of the narco gangs and stronger U.S. border security measures are cited as reasons for the decline. The sharp downturn in the U.S. economy, which struck in 2008, is also a major cause of the reduction. It is simply not as easy for a Mexican worker to find a job on the other side as it was a few years earlier.

In 2010 Mexicans threw a party for themselves. Early on the morning of September 16, 1810, Father Miguel Hidalgo issued the famous *Grito de la Independencia* (Cry of Independence, also called the Cry of Hidalgo), a stirring speech that called upon Mexicans to battle for independence from Spain. Mexican Independence Day is celebrated on September 16. It is preceded by the very special night of the *Grito*, when people gather at the town square to cheer a spokesperson who re-enacts Hidalgo's famous address. The year 2010 made for a historically important *Grito*. It marked the two hundredth anniversary of Mexican independence as well as the one hundredth birthday of the start of the Mexican Revolution of 1910-1920.

Almost a half million people crowded into the Zocalo in the heart of Mexico City on the evening of September 15, 2010, to hear President Calderón proclaim independence for the two hundredth time. Mexicans adore their fiestas. Octavio Paz said of his people, "If we hide within ourselves in our daily lives, we discharge ourselves in the whirlwind of fiesta."

The people came and cheered the floats and the marching bands as they wound around the ancient square. The country was plagued with problems: a drug war in the north and chronic poverty everywhere. Despite these troubles, Mexicans held their greatest fiesta in memory. Men and women chanted through the night: "Viva Mexico! Viva Mexico! Viva Mexico! Viva Mexico!"

Independence Day festivities in Mexico

TIMELINE

1920   General Âlvaro Obregón leads an army into Mexico City and proclaims the end of the Mexican Revolution; Obregón elected president of Mexico.

1923   Pancho Villa, a powerful general during the Revolution, ambushed and killed by gunmen in the northern Mexico town of Canutillo.

1924   Obregón's term in office expires and Plutarco Elías Calles, also an ex-army officer, becomes president.

1927   The Cristero War breaks out and as many as 80,000 Mexicans killed in the fighting.

1928   Calles steps down from office and Obregón elected to a second term as president; Obregón shot and killed days after the election by a Catholic fanatic still bitter over the Cristero War.

1928–1934   Three men serve two-year terms as president; they are president in name only as Plutarco Elías Calles is the country's true power; the press calls the three "straw men."

1934   Lázaro Cárdenas elected president.

1936   Cárdenas forces ex-president Calles to leave the country; Calles claims Mexico had fallen under the influence of communism.

1938   President Cárdenas nationalizes the oil industry and takes over all foreign oil holdings; British and American oil companies denounce the move.

1940   Leon Trotsky, a leading communist, assassinated in Mexico City; Trotsky had been close friends with Mexico's famous artist, Diego Rivera.

1941	On December 7 the Japanese bomb Pearl Harbor, plunging the United States into World War II; Mexico later joins the war on the U.S. side.
1943	U.S. President Roosevelt launches the *Bracero* Program allowing Mexican temporary laborers to cross the border and work in the United States.
1946	The *Partido Revolucionario Institucional* (the Party of Revolutionary Institutions, usually referred to by its initials PRI) established; the PRI controls the Mexican government for the remainder of the twentieth century.
1947	U.S. President Harry Truman visits Mexico City.
1950	The Mexican economy improves during a period called the "Miracle of Mexico;" tourism provides thousands of jobs.
1953	Mexican women win the right to vote.
1963	The International Olympic Committee awards the summer Olympic Games (scheduled for 1968) to Mexico City.
1968	In October, days before the Olympics, police and army officers fire at a crowd in Mexico City's Plaza of Three Cultures, killing hundreds.
1976	Mexico's foreign debt reaches $20 billion; economists warn of a crisis ahead.
1982	President Lopez Portillo announces the nationalization of all banks and the devaluation of the peso; prices for goods skyrocket and a period of terrible inflation begins.
1985	A powerful earthquake strikes Mexico City, killing at least 9,000 people; city-dwellers later complain bitterly that the army and the police force responded poorly to the emergency.

1988   Carlos Salinas de Gortari of the PRI defeats Cuauhtémoc Cárdenas in a close election for the presidency; many Mexicans claim the voting process was rigged.

1994   A peasant rebellion begins in the state of Chiapas, led by a masked man calling himself Subcomandante Marcos; the rebels call themselves the Zapatistas; Donaldo Colosio, a popular candidate for president, denounces corruption in the Mexican government and weeks later is killed by an assassin's bullet.

2000   Vicente Fox wins the election as president, breaking the decades-old grip of the PRI party; drug wars begin in northern Mexico as violent drug cartels battle each other and the police.

2010   Mexicans throw a grand fiesta to celebrate the one hundredth anniversary of the Mexican Revolution and the two hundredth birthday of independence from Spain.

SOURCES

CHAPTER ONE: Aftermath of a Revolution

p. 10,   "The chief by-product of the Revolution . . ." Frank
           Tannenbaum, *Peace By Revolution: Mexico After 1910* (New
           York: Columbia University Press, 1966), 181.

CHAPTER TWO: The Search for Stability

p. 14,   "With the hand that was . . ." Enrique Krauze, *Mexico,
           Biography of Power: A History of Modern Mexico, 1810-1996*,
           trans. Hank Heifetz (New York: Harper Collins, 1997), 386.

p. 18,   "When I was an . . ." Ibid., 405.

pp. 18-19, "I do not deny . . ." Martin Luis Guzman, *Memoirs of Pancho
           Villa* (Austin: University of Texas Press, 1966), 284.

p. 19,   "Before the uprising . . ." Ramón Eduardo Ruiz, *Triumphs
           and Tragedy: A History of the Mexican People* (New York: W. W.
           Norton & Company, 1992), 354.

p. 21,   "Here lives the president . . ." Ibid., 348.

p. 25,   "I was expelled from Mexico . . ." Jonathan Kandell, *La
           Capital: The Biography of Mexico City* (New York: Random
           House, 1988), 478.

p. 28,   "On the eighteenth of March . . ." Krauze, *Mexico, Biography
           of Power: A History of Modern Mexico, 1810-1996*, 475.

p. 29,   "the moral conscience . . ." Ibid., 480.

CHAPTER THREE: An Explosion in the Arts

p. 31,   "It is the Revolution . . ." Octavio Paz, *The Labyrinth of
           Solitude* (New York: Grove Press, 1985), 148.

p. 35,   "The painter who does not feel . . ." Kandell, *La Capital: The
           Biography of Mexico City*, 450.

p. 35,   "As far back as I can remember . . ." Pete Hamill, *Diego
           Rivera* (New York: Harry N. Abrams, Inc., 2002), 13.

p. 37,   "that the painter's scaffold . . ." Ibid., 89.

p. 40,   "the painter of the Revolution" Ruiz, *Triumphs and Tragedy: A
           History of the Mexican People*, 371.

pp. 40-41, "to produce only monumental work . . ." Ibid., 367.

p. 42,   "A curse breaks from . . ." Mariano Azuela, *The Underdogs*
           (New York: Modern Library, 2002), 148.

CHAPTER FOUR: Closer Neighbors

p. 48,   "I belong to the army . . ." Krauze, *Mexico, Biography of Power: A History of Modern Mexico, 1810-1996*, 525.

p. 48,   "I am a Catholic by origin . . . " Ibid., 506.

p. 49,   "Mexicans avoid personal dictatorships by retiring . . ." George Constable, ed. *Mexico* (New York: Time-Life Books, 1986), 139.

p. 54,   "what was good for business . . ." Ruiz, *Triumphs and Tragedy: A History of the Mexican People*, 426.

p. 55,   "It was during the Second . . ." Paz, *The Labyrinth of Solitude*, 248.

p. 56,   "There must be no illegal . . ." Krauze, *Mexico, Biography of Power: A History of Modern Mexico, 1810-1996*, 572.

p. 60,   "There are so many..." Jonathan Kandell, *La Capital: The Biography of Mexico City* (New York: Random House, 1988) 497.

p. 61,   "absolute faith in democracy . . ." Krauze, *Mexico, Biography of Power: A History of Modern Mexico, 1810-1996*, 596.

CHAPTER FIVE: The Miracle of Mexico

p. 63,   "The False Miracle," Ruiz, *Triumphs and Tragedy: A History of the Mexican People*, 410.

pp. 63-64,   "In absolute numbers . . ." Paz, *The Labyrinth of Solitude*, 259.

p. 64,   "I will not permit . . ." Krauze, *Mexico, Biography of Power: A History of Modern Mexico, 1810-1996*, 601.

p. 68,   "How could tourists . . ." Gilbert M. Joseph and Timothy J. Henderson, eds., *The Mexico Reader* (Durham: Duke University Press, 2002), 509.

p. 69,   "a poor area with a few . . ." Oscar Lewis, *The Children of Sanchez*, (New York: Vantage Books, 1963), xiii.

p. 69,   "looked thin and pale," Ibid., xviii.

pp. 69-70,   "I remember one morning . . ." Ibid., 101.

p. 73,   "They'd wrap me in cloth . . ." "Quest for the truth of torture rooms in Mexico's Black Palace," The Telegraph, http://www.telegraph.co.uk/news/worldnews/centralamericaandthecaribbean/mexico/1403644/Quest-for-truth-in-torture-rooms-of-Mexicos-Black-Palace.html.

p. 73,	"our destiny . . ." Krauze, *Mexico, Biography of Power: A History of Modern Mexico, 1810-1996*, 634.
p. 73,	"There were no polite words . . ." Ibid., 636.
p. 74,	"There was a big . . ." Ibid., 643.
p. 76,	"Do you think . . ." Ibid., 676.
p. 78,	"Come out on the balcony . . ." Kandell, *La Capital: The Biography of Mexico City*, 522.
p. 80,	"The hum of bullets . . ." Joseph and Henderson, *The Mexico Reader*, 565.
p. 80,	"The people were trampled . . ." Earl Shorris, *The Life and Times of Mexico* (New York: W. W. Norton & Company, 2004), 340.
p. 81,	"The massacre of the night . . ." Ruiz, *Triumphs and Tragedy: A History of the Mexican People*, 427.

CHAPTER SIX: Democracy and Crisis

p. 83,	"At this stage . . ." "1968: Student Riots Threaten Mexico Olympics," BBC, http://news.bbc.co.uk/onthisday/hi/dates/stories/october/2/newsid_3548000/3548680.stm.
p. 86,	"From that moment . . ." Joseph and Henderson, *The Mexico Reader*, 564.
p. 90,	"I was raised . . ." Krauze, *Mexico, Biography of Power: A History of Modern Mexico, 1810-1996*, 753.
p. 90,	"three years to pull the country . . ." Ruiz, *Triumphs and Tragedy: A History of the Mexican People*, 448.
p. 92,	"The gambler," Krauze, *Mexico, Biography of Power: A History of Modern Mexico, 1810-1996*, 753.
p. 92,	"a cheap thug," Ruiz, *Triumphs and Tragedy: A History of the Mexican People*, 448.
p. 93,	"como un perro," Krauze, *Mexico, Biography of Power: A History of Modern Mexico, 1810-1996*, 760.
p. 94,	"I was responsible . . ." Ibid.

CHAPTER SEVEN: What Went Wrong?

p. 101,	"All of a sudden . . ." Kandell, *La Capital: The Biography of Mexico City*, 568-569.
p. 104,	"This goes way beyond me . . ." Julia Preston and Samuel Dillon, *Opening Mexico: The Making of a Democracy* (New York: Farrar, Straus and Giroux, 2004), 99.
p. 104,	"The city was ours . . ." Ibid., 107.

p. 106,   "the secret religion," "The Nobel Prize in Literature 1990
            Octavio Paz: Biography," http://nobelprize.org/nobel_prizes/
            literature/laureates/1990/paz-bio.html.

CHAPTER EIGHT: **The Lure of El Norte**
p. 116,   "There's nothing slick . . ." Gilbert M. Joseph and Timothy
            J. Henderson, eds., *The Mexican Reader* (Durham: Duke
            University Press, 2002), p. 720.
p. 116,   "In the ten years . . ." Ibid., 720-721.

CHAPTER NINE: **Change and Peril**
p. 124,   "Nazism," Randall Archibold, "Arizona Enacts Stringent Law
            on Immigration," *New York Times*, April 23, 2010.
p. 126,   "This is a town without . . ." *Chicago Sun-Times*, October 21,
            2010.
p. 127,   "If we hide . . ." Paz, *The Labyrinth of Solitude*, 53.

BIBLIOGRAPHY

Camín, Héctor Aguilar. *In the Shadow of the Mexican Revolution*. Translated by Luis Albero Fierro. Austin: University of Texas Press, 1993.

Guzman, Martin Luis. *Memoirs of Pancho Villa*. Austin: University of Texas Press, 1966.

Hamill, Pete. *Diego Rivera*. New York: Harry N. Abrams, Inc., 2002.

Joseph, Gilbert M., and Timothy J. Henderson, ed. *The Mexico Reader*. Durham: Duke University Press, 2002.

Kandell, Jonathon. *La Capital: The Biography of Mexico City*. New York: Random House, 1988.

Krauze, Enrique. *Mexico, Biography of Power: A History of Modern Mexico, 1810-1996*. Translated by Hank Heifetz. New York: Harper Collins, 1997.

Lida, David. *First Stop in the New World: Mexico City, the Capital of the 21st Century*. New York: Riverhead Books, 2008.

Martinez, Ruben. *Crossing Over: A Mexican Family on the Immigrant Trail*. New York: Henry Holt, 2001.

Paz, Octavio. *The Labyrinth of Solitude*. New York: Grove Press, 1985.

Preston, Julia and Samuel Dillon. *Opening Mexico: The Making of a Democracy*. New York: Farrar, Straus and Giroux, 2004.

Raat, W. Dirk, and William H. Beezley, ed. *Twentieth Century Mexico*. Lincoln: University of Nebraska Press, 1986.

Rodriguez, Gregory. *Mongrels, Bastards, Orphans, and Vagabonds: Mexican Immigration and the Future Race in America*. New York: Vintage Books, 2007.

Ruiz, Ramón Eduardo. *Triumphs and Tragedy: A History of the Mexican People*. New York: W. W. Norton & Company, 1992.

Shorris, Earl. *The Life and Times of Mexico*. New York: W. W. Norton & Company, 2004.

Tannenbaum, Frank. *Peace By Revolution: Mexico After 1910*. New York: Columbia University Press, 1966.

Thompson, Gabriel. *There's No José Here*. New York: Nation Books, 2007.

WEB SITES

Modern Mexico Through the Eyes of Modern Mexican -
A Social History

www.mexicomike.com

The History of Mexico

www.earthyfamily.com/mexico-history.htm

The Artists as Activist: David Alfaro Siqueiros

www.mexconnect.com/... -/309-the-artist-as-activist

INDEX

PICTURE CREDITS